国家出版基金项目
NATIONAL PUBLICATION FOUNDATION

CHINESE RED
中国红

古代兵书

Ancient Books on the Art of War

王慧◎编著

全国百佳图书出版单位
ARCTIME 时代出版
时代出版传媒股份有限公司
黄山书社

图书在版编目(CIP)数据

古代兵书：汉英对照 /王慧编著. -- 合肥：黄山书社,
2013.6
（中国红）
ISBN 978-7-5461-3581-6

Ⅰ. ①古… Ⅱ. ①王… Ⅲ. ①兵法—中国—古代—汉、
英 Ⅳ. ①E892.2

中国版本图书馆CIP数据核字(2013)第098096号

古代兵书

王 慧 编著

出 版 人：任耕耘
策　　划：任耕耘　蒋一谈
责任编辑：侯　雷　李　南

特约编辑：包云鸠
装帧设计：商子庄
责任印制：戚　帅　李　磊

出版发行：时代出版传媒股份有限公司（http://www.press-mart.com）
黄山书社（http://www.hsbook.cn）
官方直营书店网址（http://hsssbook.taobao.com）
营销部电话：0551—63533762 63533768
（合肥市政务文化新区翡翠路1118号出版传媒广场7层　邮编：230071）
经　　销：新华书店
印　　刷：安徽联众印刷有限公司

开本：710×875　1/16
印张：9.75
字数：130千字
版次：2013年7月第1版
印次：2013年7月第1次印刷
书号：ISBN　978-7-5461-3581-6
定价：59.00元

前言 Preface

中国古代战争频繁，自上古时代起就不断发生战争。封建制确立之后，政权不断更迭，战争更是此起彼伏。而中国历代总结战争经验的兵书更是卷帙浩繁。历代兵书中所蕴含的内容博大精深，书中所体现的以仁为本的战争观、"知彼知己，百战不殆"的战争指导思

Since ancient times, China has witnessed consecutive and frequent wars and conflicts. With the establishment of feudalism, the war appeared to be more common due to the regime change. Meanwhile, numerous ancient canons and books on the art of war also emerged from the turmoil, in which the profound content, the kindness

想、“不战而屈人之兵”的“全胜”战略、因势用兵的作战思想和选贤任能的用将之道……共同构成了中国古代军事思想的主要内容。《孙子兵法》、《吴子兵法》、《孙膑兵法》、《武经总要》、《武备志》等著名兵书，更是为世界各国的军事家所推崇，在世界军事理论史上占据着重要的地位。

本书介绍了中国历代兵书的主要内容，简要阐述了其中所蕴含的主要军事思想，同时结合历史战役，生动形象地展示了博大精深的中国古代军事思想，向读者展现了一个充满智谋的军事天地。

oriented concept, the guiding thought of knowing the enemy and yourself, the win-win strategy of forcing enemy to retreat without a fight, the idea of deploying army according to different situation and the method of choosing appropriate officers… all make up the major content of ancient Chinese military theory. Many prestigious military canons, including *Master Sun's Art of War*, by Sun Wu, *Master Wu's Art of War*, by Wu Qi, *Sun Bin's Art of War*, by Sun Bin, *Main Points in Military Theory*, by Zeng Gongliang and Ding Du, and *Book of Military Theory*, by Mao Yuanyi, and etc., are held in considerable esteem by strategist worldwide and occupy important position in the world military theory history.

This book introduces the major theory of ancient Chinese books on art of war and briefly explains the major military thought reflected. And with the demonstration of several famous ancient battles, it exhibits the audience the extensiveness and profoundness of Chinese military theory and lively battle fields which are full of wisdom and scheme.

目 录 Contents

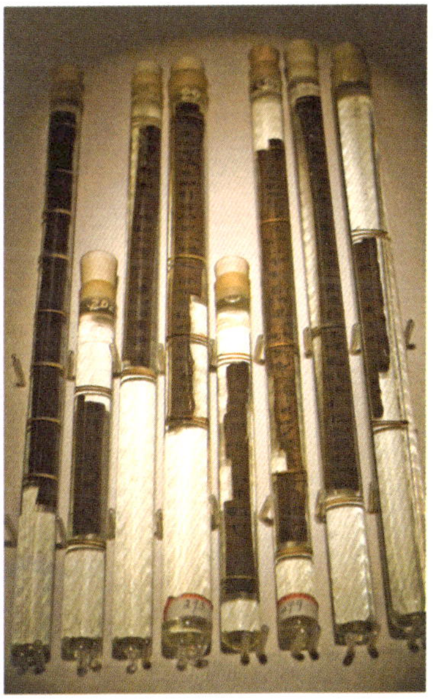

兵书的起源
Origin of the Books on the Art of War

兵书是中国古代军事著作的总称，是对古代军事斗争经验的总结。兵书的产生和其他社会事物一样，是社会发展到一定阶段的产物。在正式的兵书诞生之前，甲骨文、金文中便有了许多关于中国古代战争的记载。在此基础上，春秋战国时期产生了中国历史上最早的兵书《军志》和《军政》。

The books on the art of war is a general term of ancient Chinese military canons, also the conclusion of the experience on ancient military battles. Similar to other social matters, its origin is the product of the development of society. Before the birth of formal books on the art of war, there are many inscriptions on bones, tortoise shells or bronze articles record the ancient Chinese wars. Based on that, the earliest relevant books, *Military Strategy* and *Military Theory* appeared in the Spring and Autumn Period (770 B.C.–476 B.C.) and Warring States Period (475 B.C.–221 B.C.).

> 早期的干戈记事

在古代，由于人类的生产力低下，只有在肥沃的土地上及水域周围才能生存下去。而这样的地带又是有限的，所以便通过战争来获取

• 原始人始用兵器
Weapon Used by Ancient People

> Early Records on Wars

In ancient times, owing to the low productivity, people could only survive on the fertile soil and along the riverside. However, such area was rare and limited. So the ancient ancestor would try to obtain the fertile soil through wars and then hunt, fish and plant on these lands, which was the most primary surviving method. As it were, the war has come into being ever since the appearance of human beings.

The earliest record on wars can be found in the inscriptions on bones or tortoise shells, including Shang's attack towards the Zhou Tribe and the King of Shang's military strategies, etc.

From the establishment of the Western Zhou Dynasty (1046 B.C.-771 B.C.) to its collapse witnessed by King You of the Zhou Dynasty in 771 B.C., this country had been through many

- **利簋**

簋是中国古代用于盛放饭食的器皿。利簋又称“武王征商簋”，高28厘米，器内的底面铸有4行铭文，共32字，主要记述的是“武王伐纣”的故事。

Li Gui

Gui, is a type of food vessel in ancient China. *Li Gui*, also called *Gui* of King Wu's War Declared on Shang, with a height of 28 cm and four lines of inscriptions, totally 32 Chinese characters, at its interior bottom, which records the story of King Wu's War Declared on King Zhou.

肥沃的土地，进而在这些土地上狩猎、捕鱼、耕种，这是早期人类最基本的生存方式。可以说，从有人类开始便有了战争。

中国最早关于战争的记载可以在甲骨文上找到，例如关于商王令军队去进攻周族的记载、关于商王率军布阵打仗的记载等。

公元前11世纪，西周王朝建立，直到公元前771年周幽王丧国，期间经历了许多著名的战争。这一时期，中国的青铜器铸造非常兴盛，人们开始在铜器上用金文记录战争。

记录战争的金文以利簋铭文最为著名。利簋铭文所记载的内容大致为：一天清晨，天还没有亮，周

famous battles and wars. In this period, due to the blooming of the production of bronze articles, people started to record the wars in the inscriptions on the bronze articles.

The most famous bronze ware inscription about the battle is the one on *Li Gui* (a round-mouthed food vessel with two or four loop handles), which is quoted as: one day in the morning, when the day was still dark, King Wu of State Zhou sent the army to attack Shang's city and defeated the fatuous King of Shang Dynasty, Zhou. It was one of the most prestigious battles in Chinese history, called Battle of Muye. In the late Shang Dynasty (1600 B.C.-1046 B.C.), King Wu led his army and arrived at Muye (today's southwest area of Qi County of

牧野之战（图片提供：微图）
Battle of Muye

武王便派遣军队征讨商朝，并且战胜了昏庸的商王。这段记述描写的是中国历史上最著名的战役之一——牧野之战。在商朝末年，周武王率军进抵牧野（今河南淇县西南），商纣王派守卫国都的军队及临时强迫征来的大批奴隶迎战。武王严阵誓师，激励部众斗志，而纣王阵中的奴隶却纷纷倒戈。武王乘胜追击，商军大败，纣王逃回朝歌，随后自焚。武王占领了商都，灭亡了商朝（前1600—前1046），结束了商纣王昏庸的统治。

Henan Province), while King Zhou of the Shang Dynasty was forced to summon the city defending troop and bunches of salves to resist the attack. King Wu took a mass pledge at the front and inspired his followers. On the other hand, King Zhou's slave soldiers defected one after another. King Wu chased Shang's troop in the field and King Zhou fled back to his city Zhaoge and burned himself in his own courtyard. King Wu took the city and declared the end of the Shang Dynasty and the tyranny of the King Zhou.

甲骨文与金文

甲骨文是商周时期刻在龟甲、兽骨上的文字，是中国早期的象形文字，图画性比较强，现今共发现有4500字左右。

金文，又称“铭文”，是铸刻在商周青铜器上的文字。金文大都是铸出来的（少数是刻），一般铸于青铜器之上。西周时期的钟、鼎、乐器、食器、兵器等青铜器上，可以见到精美的铭文，所以金文又有“钟鼎文”之称。

Bone Inscriptions and Bronze Ware Inscriptions

Bone inscriptions indicate the primitive characters carved on tortoise shells and animal bones in the Shang and Zhou dynasties(1600 B.C.-256 B.C.). It is the early hieroglyphics in China with a strong graphic feature. So far, there are about 4,500 characters found in total.

Bronze ware inscriptions, also called epigraph, indicate the characters carved on bronze ware. The most of them were cast out of its mould and only seldom were carved out. They mainly appear on the bronze ware of the Shang and Zhou dynasties(1600 B.C.-256 B.C.), including bell (*Zhong*), *Ding* (ancient cooking vessel), musical instruments, food vessels, weapons and etc., in the Western Zhou Dynasty (1046 B.C.-771 B.C.). So it is also called Zhongding Inscriptions.

• 刻在兽骨上的甲骨文

Bone Inscriptions on the Animal Bone

• 西周史墙盘铭文拓片

Rubbing of Bronze Plate Inscriptions Produced by Official Historian Qiang (Western Zhou Dynasty, 1046 B.C.-771 B.C.)

青铜器过伯簋上的铭文记录了周昭王南征之战。过伯簋约铸于周昭王十六年（前980），系方座簋，高18.4厘米，器内铸铭文16字，记载了过伯随周昭王攻伐荆楚的史实。周昭王十六年（前980），昭王率领众将进攻南方的荆楚（今湖北）。荆楚等诸侯国和族军在汉水南岸布设防御工事，想利用天然的水屏障来阻击周军。周军过江后，下令将船凿破，以示不获全胜绝不收兵。昭王获胜后因无船可用，便限令当地船夫在3日内制造可供15000人渡江的船只。船夫由于难以完成，便将以前的破船用胶粘合。当周军渡

The bronze ware Guobo *Gui* records the Southern Campaign Led by King Zhao of the Zhou Dynasty in 980 B.C., which was cast with a square base, with a height of 18.4 cm and 16 characters inscribed on the interior describing a fragment story of Guobo following King Zhao's army to launch a strike over Jingchu area. In 980 B.C., King Zhao of the Zhou Dynasty initiated a war opposed to the vassal states in Jingchu area (today's Hubei Province). And the local soldiers set series of defense fortifications along the southern bank of Han River in order to resist Zhou's attack depending on its natural terrain. After Zhou's army across the river, King Zhao ordered to sink all the ships to express his determination for victory. So when King Zhao won the war, he had no ship

周昭王像

周昭王（？–前977），西周第四代国王。

Portrait of King Zhao of the Zhou Dynasty

King Zhao of the Zhou Dynasty (?-977 B.C.), is the fourth King of the Western Zhou Dynasty (1046 B.C.-771 B.C.).

• 班簋
Ban Gui

to employ. So he ordered the local boatman to build the ships for 15,000 soldiers within three days. As it was an impossible mission, the boatman was forced to use glue to stick the former sunk wreckages together. While Zhou's army crossed the river, the glue was melted and most of the boats sank in the river. At this time, the joint troop of Jingchu seized the opportunity and chased out the Zhou's army.

江时，胶着水溶化，大多沉没，荆楚联军乘机出击，大败周军。

The bronze ware *Ban Gui* records the Battle to Dongyi (general term for ethnic groups living in the eastern areas of China) led by King Cheng of the Zhou Dynasty with detailed description. In the August, King Cheng appointed Maobo Ban to launch a strike over Dongyi people with the troop made up by the imperial army dispatched from Shaanxi Province and also the vassal armies as well as the troop from the near State Wu and State Lü. During this war, Maobo Ban made a thorough plan and logical deploy. In three years, he finally won the war.

而青铜器班簋的铭文则记载了周成王征东夷之战，并详细记载了周成王下令征伐东夷（中国东部民族的泛称）的经过。某年八月，周成王命令毛伯班征伐东夷。这次战争出动的武装力量，既有从数千里外的陕西调来的王室军队，又有相距较远的诸侯国军队，还有就近的吴国和吕国的军队。其间毛伯班运筹决策、计划部署，经过三年征战，终于告捷。

> 最早的兵书

中国古代兵书的内容十分丰富，种类繁多。虽然哪一本是最早的兵书目前尚不能确定，但还是能够从春秋战国（前770—前221）以来的《左传》、《孙子兵法》等文献中找到一些早期兵书的内容。《军志》和《军政》一直被认为是中国最早的兵书，但是这两种兵书早已失传，只是在后来的史籍中还保留着一些片断。据研究，这两部兵书大致是西周晚期的作品。《军志》和《军政》的内容丰富，不仅仅有对军事活动的简单记载，还总结和概括了一些军事活动的经验，并在一定程度上揭示了战争和军事活动中的某些规律。

《军志》的内容现已发现的有七则，其中在《左传》中有三则，

> Earliest Books on the Art of War

The content of books on the art of war in ancient China is rich and diversified. Although the first book on the art of war can not be confirmed yet, several records about the early books on the art of war still can be found in the literatures, such as *The Commentary of Zuo* and *Master Sun's Art of War* written since the Spring and Autumn Period (770 B.C.-476 B.C.). *Military Strategy* and *Military Theory* have been considered as the earliest works. However, they had been long gone. Only some fragments of records can prove its existence. According to the research, the two books were approximately written in the late Western Zhou Dynasty (1046 B.C.-771 B.C.). They have ample content and not only are the simple record on military activities but also conclude the relevant experience

• 商代战车（模型）
Model of Chariot in the Shang Dynasty

在《十一家注孙子》中有两则，在《太平御览》中有一则，在《通典》中有一则。

《左传》中第一则的主要内容为"允当则当"、"知难而退"、"有德不可敌"。具体含义是：在达到了一定的军事目的后，要即时停止军事活动，不要无限地扩展军事行动；同时，军事行动要审时度势，如果真的遇到了困难，要正视困难，并及时撤退；最后，强调

and reveal some regular patterns in these activities.

Now, seven fragments of the content of *Military Strategy* now have been found in several ancient canons: three in *The Commentary of Zuo*, two in the *Master Sun's Art of War Commented by Eleven Scholars*, one in the *Taiping Imperial Encyclopaedia*, and one in the *General Canon*.

The first rule quoted in *The Commentary of Zuo* indicates that the

了德行的重要性，并认为有德行的国家是不可战胜的。把德政作为决定战争胜负的首要条件，是当时军事家难能可贵的思想。

《左传》中第二则的主要内容是“先人有夺人之心”。这句话的含义是：先发制人是作战中战胜他人所应有的一种观念。春秋时期，楚国便是在该思想的指导下，先发制人，大获全胜，从晋国手中夺得了中原霸权。

• 西周早期的鹰首短剑

Early Eagle Hilt Dagger (Western Zhou Dynasty, 1046 B.C.-771 B.C.)

military activity should stop when it suffices and shrink back when it gets stuck and the idea that the country who values the morality shall never be defeated, meaning: once achieved the purpose, the leader should cease the attack and do not expand the activity blindly; and the leader should be sensible and can face the difficulty directly and pull back in time as a expedient; and in the last, it emphasizes the importance of the morality and explains the country who values the morality shall never be defeated. This thought that weighs the benevolent rule over the result of battles was very rare at that time.

The second rule quoted in *The Commentary of Zuo* indicates that the strategy of taking the first step is a necessary concept. In the Spring and Autumn Period (770 B.C.-476 B.C.), under the guidance of this strategy, the State Chu took the supremacy from the State Jin over a great victory.

The third rule quoted in *The Commentary of Zuo* usually employed with the second rule above, indicates that despite the failure in the strategy of taking the first step, another remedy of waiting for the later attack while the enemy was vulnerable can also turn the

• 西周早期的青铜兵器——戈

Bronze Weapon: Dagger-axe (*Ge*) in the Early Western Zhou Dynasty(1046 B.C.-771 B.C.)

《左传》中第三则的内容与第二则相互呼应，为“后人有待其衰”。其意思是：如果作战时我们真的做不到先发制人，这也并不意味着失败，还可以采用一种补救的办法，即后发制人。但后发制人一定要把握好一个条件，那就是在敌人的士气衰竭的时候才出兵。

《十一家注孙子》中包含两则内容，第一则的主要内容为“止则为营，行则为阵”。意思是说军队在夜晚停止行进时要扎营，聚集在一起；行进时要遵守严格的军事纪律，时刻保持警惕，随时能转换为战阵。第二则的内容主要是要求领兵的将帅把战阵部署得天衣无缝，在各种情况下都能自如地击破敌军。

《太平御览》中的那则的内容

table. However, the timing is everything. The attack should be launched when the opponent's momentum is low.

There are two rules quoted in the *Master Sun's Art of War Commented by Eleven Scholars*. The first one tells that in the night, the troop should stop marching and build camp to take a rest together; and in the day, the troop should abide by the military discipline strictly and keep alert all the time to prepare for change of battle array. The second one tells that the leader should have a thorough plan which is able to sever the opponent under any circumstances.

The main content quoted in *Taiping Imperial Encyclopaedia*, includes three points: confidentiality, solidarity and speed, meaning: leaders should have a strong sense of confidentiality while making plans and arranging the

是“三要”，即要保密、要团结、要速战。意思是统兵将帅要有极强的保密观念，在制定作战计划、进行军事部署时要严格保密，不可泄露军机；统兵将帅要采用各种措施，使部队上下团结一心、一致对敌；统兵将帅在指挥部队作战时，军令要威严如山，行动要迅雷不及掩耳，这样才能使敌人主帅的决策来不及实施。

《通典》中的那则主要强调了“地利”的重要性。即军队作战时，一旦失去了有利的地形条件，兵士就会迷惑，怀疑战争是否还可以取胜。而且失去了地利，军队行进将会困难重重，最终必会导致失败。

deployment; and they also should adopt all the measures to make the troop united and determined for the victory; and while commanding the soldiers, the orders should be observed strictly and carried out rapidly in order to response the scheme employed by the opponent ahead of the time.

In *General Canon*, it mainly emphasizes the importance of the advantage of a favorable terrain: once the army loses the advantage of the terrain, the soldiers will become confused and start to have a doubt on the victory, and also the marching of the troop will become difficult and dangerous, which will finally lead to the failure.

The record on the content of *Military*

• 西周时的作战场景
Battlefield (Western Zhou Dynasty, 1046 B.C.-771 B.C.)

• **古代战场上的军旗**（图片提供：微图）
Army Flag in Ancient Battlefield

《军政》的内容保留下来的较少，目前能见到两则。第一则为"言不相闻，故为之金鼓；视不相见，故为之旌旗"。主要是讲在行军不利的条件下，要想方法引导和促进行军和指导战争。例如，如果军队因过于庞大、相互间距离较远而听不见将领言语上的指挥，那么可以通过设置锣鼓等听觉信号向士兵们传递信息；如果军队过于庞大或将领相对较矮，士兵们看不到将

Theory is rare. So far, there are two rules preserved. The first is to tell that under the disadvantages of communicating with the soldiers, the leader should take the relevant methods to guide the troop and to encourage the soldiers. For example, if the army is too large that the military officers in the distance can not hear each other, then they can set gong and drum as the audible signal to send message to the soldiers; if the army is large and the leader is relatively short, so that the

领的行动指挥，那么可以通过设置一些旌旗等视觉信号来指挥军队。这些做法可以使军队在行进的过程中仍保持严明的纪律，保持所有人的动作一致，保证战争在将领的指挥下有序进行。第二则为“见可而进，知难而退”。主要是讲战无常法，在作战时一定要根据实际情况采取措施。遇到有利的条件就应迅速进攻敌人，遇到不利条件就要及时撤退。

soldiers can not see his hand signal, then he can use several banners or flags as the visible signal to guide the troop. These measures can guarantee the discipline is strictly followed and the actions are consistent and the orders are carried out sequentially. The second is to tell that there are no common rules about war. In the battlefield, one should alter the strategy on the basis of the situation. When having the advantages, the attack should be launched rapidly; when having the disadvantages, the retreat should be instructed in time.

淝水之战——《军政》“见可而进”思想的运用

“见可而进”指的是统帅将领经过对敌我双方军事诸条件的分析后，如得出我优敌劣的结论，就可以果断做出对敌发起进攻的决定，借以取得战争的胜利。

淝水之战是东晋军在淝水（今安徽省境内）击败前秦军的一场大战，是中国历史上以少胜多的著名战役，也是“见可而进”作战思想的完美运用。公元383年，前秦为了扩张领土而对东晋发动了大规模的进攻。面对前秦的进攻，东晋宰相谢安经过分析比较，认为前秦军队大多是沿途招募的新兵，数量虽多，但大都为乌合之众。且前秦军内部不稳定，纪律松弛，主将骄傲无谋，因此可以进行反击。果真，在淝水之战中，东晋以八万军力战胜了前秦八十七万大军。

战国铜器纹饰中的射箭图

Pattern Describing Several Archers on a Bronze Ware (Warring States Period, 475 B.C.-221 B.C.)

战国铜器纹饰中的攻战图

Pattern Describing an Ancient Battlefield on a Bronze Ware (Warring States Period, 475 B.C.-221 B.C.)

Battle of Feishui: Attack Under the Advantages, from *Military Theory*

The theory of attack under the advantages indicates that after a thorough analysis on several conditions for both sides, if the leader can get a result of having advantages over the enemy, then he can launch the attack immediately to win the battle.

The Battle of Feishui is a famous and typical battle of defeating the enemy with a force inferior in number in Chinese history. It was between the Eastern Jin Dynasty (317-420) and the State of Former Qin at the southeastern area of Shouxian County in Anhui Province. It was also a perfect example for the theory of attack under the advantages. In 383, in order to expand the territory, the State of Former Qin struck a war to the Eastern Jin Dynasty with a large troop. Facing the attack, the Prime Minister of the Eastern Jin Dynasty, Xie An pointed out that despite the large number, the troop of the Former Qin was mostly recruited along its marching, who was not capable of the fight in the battlefield, additionally, the lack of stability and discipline and the arrogance of the leader were its Achilles' heel. So he stood for the counterattack. As expected, in this battle, Eastern Jin Dynasty defeated the attack with a force of 80,000 soldiers against Former Qin's 870,000.

历代兵书

Books on the Art of War Through History

自春秋末期至清朝末年的2500多年中，中华民族涌现出了许多杰出的军事家和兵书著述家。他们所著的兵书浩如烟海，构成了中国古代军事文化的重要内容，成为人们研究中国古代军事思想的文献宝库。

Within the 2,500 years of history from the late Spring and Autumn Period (770 B.C.–476 B.C.) and to the late Qing Dynasty (1644–1911), there appeared numerous outstanding strategists and writers of the books on the art of war. These countless canons and masterpieces constitute an important part of ancient Chinese military culture and have become the treasury of the references for people's study on ancient Chinese military theories.

>《孙子兵法》

《孙子兵法》是中国现存最早的兵书，成书于春秋末年。该书是一部内容完备、结构严谨的军事名著，它的产生为中国军事学的发展奠定了坚实的基础。孙武把与战争有关的军事问题分作十三篇加以论述，全书有完整的理论体系和新颖独特的论述形式，被誉为“世界第一兵书”。

《孙子兵法》中，“慎战”思想及关于战争指导原则的“全胜”理论是全书的精华所在。在该兵书问世之后，得到了社会普遍的重视和赞誉，作者孙武被推崇为兵学的鼻祖。

《孙子兵法》不仅仅是中国兵书宝库中的瑰宝，在世界上也广为流传。它于8世纪传入日本，18世纪

> Master Sun's Art of War

Master Sun's Art of War, by Sun Wu is the earliest book on the art of war, which was written in the late Spring and Autumn Period (770 B.C.-476 B.C.). It is a masterpiece with complete content and rigorous structure. Its appearance has laid a firm foundation for the development of Chinese military science. With thirteen chapters, this book has an intact theoretical system and original narration, which makes it the Top Book on the Art of War in the World.

In *Master Sun's Art of War*, the thought of being cautious in war and the guiding principle of a complete victory are the essence of the whole book. It was highly praised after being known by the public and the writer Sun Wu was also held in esteem as the Founder of Strategics.

The *Master Sun's Art of War* is not

《孙子兵法》竹简（图片提供：微图）
Bamboo Slips of *Master Sun's Art of War*

传入欧洲，现今已被翻译成多种文字。在海湾战争中，美国军官人手一册英文版的《孙子兵法》和一盘解释《孙子兵法》的录音带。

作者简介

孙武，又称“孙子”，字长卿，春秋时期的齐国人，中国古代伟大的军事家和军事理论家，被后人奉为“兵圣”。

出身于军功贵族世家的孙武积累了许多军事方面的实战经验，为他后来研究兵法、著述兵书及在战

only a treasury of Chinese military theory but also a monumental work in the world. It was introduced into Japan in the 8th century and then into Europe in the 18th century. Now, it has been translated into multiple languages around the world. In the Gulf War, all the American officers got a copy of the English version and a tutoring tape for them to study.

Biography

Sun Wu, also addressed Sun Zi, with the courtesy name of Changqing, was a citizen from the State Qi in the Spring

• 孙武像
Portrait of Sun Wu

争中建功立业，奠定了良好的基础。吴王阖闾当政时期（前514—前496），孙武被吴王重用为将，曾带兵三万与二十万楚兵相战，几次打败楚国，终于在公元前506年攻陷楚国的都城郢（今湖北荆州市荆州区西北）。当时的吴国兴盛一时，可以与北方强国齐、晋相抗衡，这些功业都与孙武的贡献有直接的关系。

主要军事思想

《孙子兵法》开篇指出：战争是“国之大事”，它关系到国家的

and Autumn Period (770 B.C.-476 B.C.). He was a great strategist and military theorist in ancient China and was held in esteem as the Sage of Strategics.

He was born in a decorated noble family and had accumulated much military experience in practice, which laid a good foundation for his future study, writing and achievement in the battles. In the reign of King Helü of the State Wu (514 B.C.-496 B.C.), Sun Wu was appointed as the general by the king and once led 30,000 soldiers to resist a troop of 200,000 soldiers of the State Chu and repetitively won the battles. Finally, in 506 B.C., he took the capital city Ying (today's northwest area of Jingzhou District, Jingzhou City, Hubei Province) of the State Chu. Then the State Wu reached its great prosperity and was able to contend against the State Qi and State Jin in the north. These accomplishments could never be achieved without the contribution of Sun Wu.

Major Military Theory

In the beginning of the book *Master Sun's Art of War*, it points out that: war is of great significance to the country. It relates to the destiny of the country

存亡和人民的生死，因此必须慎重对待，深思熟虑，周详计算。这便是他著名的“慎战”思想。

关于战争的最佳状态是什么，不同的军事家有不同的理解。孙武认为战争的最佳状态是军事家运用高超的谋略破坏敌人的战略企图，使之不攻自破；或运用外交手段瓦解敌人的外交联盟，争取更多的盟国，使敌人孤立无援，从外交上战胜敌人。这便是“不战而屈人之兵”的思想。综合起来，即以武力为后盾，以谋略、外

• 春秋吴王光剑

Sword Belonging to King Guang of the State Wu (Spring and Autumn Period, 770 B.C.-476 B.C.)

and its people, so the war should be deliberately weighed and considered with thorough and meticulous plan. This is the famous theory of being cautious in war.

According to the definition of the best circumstance in a war, different strategists usually have various understandings. Sun Wu believed that the best circumstance is to defeat the enemy by sabotaging the opponent's scheme with a better strategy and leaving it collapsing on its own, or to exert the diplomacy to alienate the enemy's alliance and earn more supporters to make them alone and abandoned. This is the thought of the win-win strategy of forcing enemy to retreat without a fight. In conclusion, a country should see its military force as a backup and try to trade for the victory of the largest with strategy and diplomacy.

Sun Wu also asserted that people should weigh the war on five perspectives called Five Issues, namely public opinion, weather or climate, terrain, military officer and discipline. The first one is the public opinion, meaning if the king wants to launch a war, he must make sure that his people and officials are united and the government is of integrity; weather or climate indicates the climate conditions;

交等为手段，用最小的代价换取最大的胜利。

孙武还主张应从五个方面来考量一场战争，即道、天、地、将、法，称“五事”。“五事”中居于第一位的是“道”，道即“令民与上同意”，即要进行征战，首先必须国内上下同心，政治清明。“天”指气候、时令等方面的条件。“地”指作战时的地形、地势的条件。“将”是指挥战争的将领，孙子认为将领必须具备五个方面的素质，即智慧、诚信、仁义、勇敢和严明。“法”指军队建制、管理方式和作战指挥制度等方面。孙武将训练有素、令行禁止、战斗力强大的精兵看成是决定战争胜负的决定性因素，这也是孙武治军思想的核心。

除了“五事”，孙武还提出了“知彼知己，百战不殆”的思想。即只有靠切实的侦查研究，全面掌握敌我双方力量的对比，才能扬长避短，在战斗中获得主动权，而争取主动权是达到“全胜”的必要条件。

孙武认为，灵活多变的战法是达到“全胜”的重要手段。即正确

terrain indicates the geographical condition in the battle field; military officer indicates the leader of the battle who should process five elements, namely wisdom, sincerity, kindheartedness, valiance and seriousness; discipline indicates the organizational system of the army, the management style and the rules of operational command. In his opinion, the well-trained soldier, strict discipline, strict enforcement of orders, and high fighting capacity are the determining factors of the final victory, which is also the core of Sun Wu's theory.

Aside from the Five Issues, Sun Wu also raised the thought that: knowing yourself as well as the enemy can then keep you in an invincible position, which takes cogent investigation and study to be fully aware of the situation of the military forces from both sides, thereby exerting advantages and avoiding the disadvantages, in order to take the initiative in the war. And the initiative is the necessary requirement to attain the complete victory.

Sun Wu believes that the flexible strategy is a significant method to achieve the complete victory. While fighting against odds, the appropriate deployment and flexible strategy can distract the

"以寡敌众"法应用于中医配药

清代名医徐大椿借用《孙子兵法》的用兵之道，提出了"用药如用兵"论。如将"以寡敌众"法（能战胜敌人就与敌人进行战争，不能战胜敌人就选择回避战争，迂回作战）应用到治病中，提出对于较为严重的疾病，可采用将病症分解的方法进行治疗，阶段性一步步治疗，最终便可治愈。

Theory of Fight Against Odds Applied in the Prescription Making in Traditional Chinese Medicine

In the Qing Dynasty (1644-1911), a famous doctor Xu Dachun was inspired by the military theory stated in *Master Sun's Art of War*, and proposed a theory that making prescription is like deploying the army. As to the theory of fight against odds (under adverse circumstances, one should avoid the direct conflict with the enemy and take the detour to resist; otherwise, one can take the direct hit if capable), it was applied in his medical theory to deal with the severe disease by decomposing the symptoms and treating them one by one.

• 中药
Traditional Chinese Medicine

春秋铜胄

Bronze Helmet (Spring and Autumn Period, 770 B.C.-476 B.C.)

使用兵力和灵活多变的战法，如在以少敌多的情况下，可以先采取各种办法使敌人兵力分散，然后集中优势兵力战胜敌人，这就是“避实而击虚”的道理。

孙武主张，战争中不要做意气之争，在敌人气势旺盛、势力强大的时候要暂避其锋芒，等到敌人懈怠麻痹的时候再出其不意地战胜敌人。因此，战争中要耐心等待敌人弱点的暴露，只要全面地掌握敌人的真实情况，就一定可以找到敌人的薄弱环节进行攻击。

opponent's force and then concentrate a superior force to give the enemy a final strike. It is the thought of avoiding the strong and attacking the weak.

Sun Wu believes that arrogance can be very dangerous in the battle field. When the enemy is in unstoppable momentum, one should avoid the direct conflict and wait until the enemy becomes sloppy, then launch a surprise raid on them. Therefore, the leader should wait until the opponent exposes its weakness. As long as fully understanding the real situation of the enemy, one can find the vulnerable part to attack.

《孙子兵法》的完美运用——赤壁之战

中国古典名著《三国演义》中的“火烧赤壁”是书中最为著名的片断之一，所描述的内容是中国古代历史上著名的战争——赤壁之战。赤壁之战发生于东汉建安十三年（208），孙权和刘备联军在长江的赤壁一带与曹操军队展开决战，这场战役是对《孙子兵法》的完美运用。孙刘联军在敌强我弱、敌众我寡的形势下，利用我方熟悉水战的优势，避实击虚，采取火攻的计策，烧毁曹军战船，从而大破曹军。

A Perfect Example of the Implementation of *Master Sun's Art of War*: Battle of Chibi (Red Cliff)

As one of the Four Great Classical Novels in China, *Romance of the Three Kingdoms* has a famous story: Fire at Chibi (Red Cliff), which describes one of the most prestigious battles in ancient Chinese history: Battle of Chibi. It happened in 208, the joint army of Sun Quan and Liu Bei tried to resist the large army led by Cao Cao. This battle is a perfect example of the implementation of *Master Sun's Art of War*. Despite their numerical disadvantage, the joint army depending on their rich experience in water battle avoided the direct confrontation and applied the fire attack to burn down Cao Cao's warships and finally won the battle.

• 赤壁之战
Battle of Chibi

《吴子兵法》

《吴子兵法》是与《孙子兵法》齐名的古代兵书，成书于战国前期。它继承和发展了《孙子兵法》的有关思想，总结了战国前期的战争经验和特点，受到后世兵家的重视。该兵书的军事理论以“内修文德，外治武备”为核心而自成体系，其主要思想有三：其一是严明治军，其二是料敌用兵，其三是因敌而战。具有鲜明的时代特色。

《吴子兵法》问世后，不但在国内与《孙子兵法》一起被后人称为“孙吴兵法”，也是最早传至世界其他国家的兵书之一，对中外军事文化的交流产生了深远的影响。

作者简介

吴起（？—前381）是战国前期

Master Wu's Art of War

Master Wu's Art of War, written in the early Warring States Period (475 B.C.-221 B.C.) is a famous ancient book on the art of war, having a same position with *Master Sun's Art of War*. It has inherited and developed the theory in the *Master Sun's Art of War* and concluded the military experience and characteristics at that time. Therefore, it has been highly praised by the later generations. The military theory of this book is an original system with the core thought of cultivating the literary virtue on the interior and managing the military affairs on the exterior. It includes three major principles: the first is to strictly carry out the order; the second is to apply different strategies based on various situations; the third is to attack when the enemy is vulnerable. This book is epochal and distinctive among others.

吴起与河西之战

吴起的一生中，所立战功无数，河西之战便是他的重要功绩之一。公元前409年，魏王任命吴起为主将，在准备比较充分的情况下攻陷了秦国五城，攻取了秦军占领的河西地区，使“秦兵不敢东向”。

Wu Qi and Battle of Hexi

In Wu Qi's decorated life, the Battle of Hexi was one of his most important achievements. In 409 B.C., the king of the State Wei appointed Wu Qi as the general to strike an attack to five cities of the State Qin in advance preparation. They took the Hexi area and deterred the Qin's army from expanding eastward.

• 吴起像
Portrait of Wu Qi

After the appearance of *Master Wu's Art of War*, not only was it called Sun Wu (two characters representing their surnames) Military Books along with *Master Sun's Art of War*, but also was one of the famous military books introduced to other countries in the early days, which exerted profound influence on the communication between China and foreign countries.

Biography

Wu Qi (?-381 B.C.), was an outstanding political reformer and strategist. As his

著名的政治改革家和军事家，因其所著的兵学经典《吴子兵法》在兵法理论上有独到之处，后人将其与孙武并称“孙吴”。吴起从小就志存高远，一心想建功立业。他一生历仕鲁国、魏国和楚国，以文韬武略振兴三国，使三国出现了“吴起在而兴盛，吴起去而衰亡”的“吴起现象”。

military canon is distinctive in theories, later people call him and Sun Wu as Sun Wu (two characters representing their surnames). Ever since his childhood, Wu Qi was very ambitious and always wanted to make achievements. He served in three states: State Lu, State Wei and State Chu. He helped three states reached their prosperity. And when he left, they all declined to some extent.

主要军事思想

吴起的治军思想是与他的治国思想相结合的，而他所有关于军事问题的论述都是围绕着他治国的根本目的“内修文德，外治武备”而展开的。“文德”是指道、义、礼、仁等政治所涵盖的基本内容；“武备”是指使国家安定强盛的军事实力。如果国家的文德好，用仁、义来教育百姓，用德、礼来熏陶民众，用贤能的人来治理国家，那么百姓就能安居乐业，民众就会拥护国家。要达到国家的武备，则要招募有才能的将领，建设强大的军队，以守卫和壮大国家，防止突发事件。

吴起不主张频繁地发动战争。

Major Military Theory

Wu Qi's military theory closely relates to his governing thought. All of the discussions about military issues center on his fundamental objective of cultivating the literary virtue on the interior and managing the military affairs on the exterior in state management. The literary virtue indicates the basic content of morality, righteousness, manner, and benevolence. And military affairs indicate the powerful military force which can maintain the national stability. If the state emphasizes the literary virtue and uses benevolence and righteousness to educate its people, it will earn their support. If the state wants to obtain a powerful military force, it should recruit talented officers to build a formidable army in the purpose

• **战国双环首云纹铜剑**

Bronze Dagger with Cloud Pattern and Double-ring Hilt (Warring States Period, 475 B.C.-221 B.C.)

• **战国铜斧**

Bronze Axe (Warring States Period, 475 B.C.-221 B.C.)

• **战国铜钺**

钺是中国古代的一种两角上翘、具有弧形阔刃的劈砍兵器。

Bronze Battle-axe (*Yue*) (Warring States Period, 475 B.C.-221 B.C.)

Battle-axe is an ancient Chinese weapon with two tips cocking up and having an arc-shaped broad blade.

“内修文德”的体现——刘邦约法三章

刘邦（前256或前247—前195）是汉朝的开国皇帝。他在带兵刚入咸阳（秦国都城）时，就废除了繁杂残酷的秦律，并“约法三章”（杀人者要处死，伤人者要抵罪，盗窃者也要判罪），赢得了人民的信任和拥护，最终得到了天下。“约法三章”充分体现了他对民心的重视，这也是《吴子兵法》中“内修文德”的充分体现。

Cultivating the Literary Virtue on the Interior: Liu Bang’s Three Laws

Liu Bang (256 B.C. or 247 B.C.-195 B.C.), was the founder of the Han Dynasty (206 B.C.-220 A.D.). When he entered Xianyang(Qin’s capital city), he abolished the tedious and cruel laws and issued Three Laws (murderers should be sentenced to death; attempt murderers should be punished for his crime; thieves should be punished for his crime too) and earned people’s trust and support and finally conquer the whole country. The Three Laws reflect his concern for the welfare of the people, which is also an example for cultivating the literary virtue on the interior emphasized in *Master Wu’s Art of War*.

• 刘邦称帝

Liu Bang’s Ascending the Throne

他认为，天下从事战争的国家，五战五胜的，会招来祸患；四战四胜的，会国力疲敝；三战三胜的，可以称霸；二战二胜的，可以称王；一战一胜的，才能成就帝业。取得战争胜利容易，但是保存胜利的成果却是不容易的，因此国家要重视礼义，不要轻易发动战争。

吴起认为，治军应“以治为胜”、“教戒为先”。军队只有具备严明的军纪，上行下效，才能在

of national security and further expansion and prevention for emergency.

Wu Qi believes the state should avoid repetitive wars. He thinks if the state triumphs for five times, it will provoke disasters; if the state triumphs for four times, it will be exhausted; if the state triumphs for three times, it can seize the hegemony; if the state triumphs for twice, it can claim the throne; if the state triumphs for once, it can establish an empire. It is easy to win a battle, but it is

• 古代军队宿营图
Ancient Military Camp

战争中取得胜利。治军的关键在于治将，应选拔文武相济、决策果断、战法多变、刚柔兼备的人担任统兵将领。同时还必须要有一支纪律严明、训练有素的精兵，能够在驻营时遵守纪律，行军时威武雄壮，进攻时敌不能挡，退却时敌不能追等。

《吴子兵法》关于“料敌”用兵的论述主要集中在《料敌》篇中，针对齐、秦、楚、燕、韩、赵等六国的不同国情，提出了不同的作战方针和战法。“料敌用兵”是指在战争中，将领不仅要根据自己军队的状况，更要详细参考和考虑敌军的状况，进而来决定用兵的策略。例如对于君臣骄奢、政令松弛、军心不一的齐国，可采用兵分三路的策略大举进攻；对于国势强盛、政令严明、赏罚有信的秦国，要先以利诱导，待其士卒失去控制时乘机袭击；对于国势衰弱、国土广阔、政令紊乱、人民疲困的楚国，应先袭击其驻地，挫伤其士气，再以骑兵突击，速进速退，不断消耗他们的士气，便可取胜。

吴起还主张因敌而战，即查明

difficult to maintain the victorious result. Therefore, the state should emphasize the importance of manner and righteousness and do not launch the war easily.

Wu Qi believes that military management should follow the thought of setting strict disciplines first. As long as there are strict disciplines which are abode by all the soldiers and officers, the army can win in the battle. And the key point in the military management is the officer. The leader should appoint the officer who is adept with both the pen and the sword, resolute in decision making and resourceful in strategy planning. Meanwhile, there should be a well-trained troop with strict discipline, who can follow the discipline while setting camp and be valiant while marching and be unstoppable while attacking and be motive while retreating.

In *Master Wu's Art of War*, the discussion on applying different strategies based on various situations, specifically the states of Zhao, Qin, Chu, Yan, Han and Zhao, mainly collected in the chapter of *Strategy Plan*. It tells that the officer should not only choose the tactic according to the situation of the army of his own but also refer it of

• **战国皮甲胄**

Leather Armor (Warring States Period, 475 B.C.-221 B.C.)

敌人实力的虚实，在敌人处于危机时与敌人作战。他提出了八种敌人处于危机时的情况，例如当敌人在严寒酷暑的条件下行军时、粮草和物资即将耗尽时、兵力不足时、救兵未到时等。

the enemy. For example, as for the plan toward to State Qi in which the king is arrogant and the administration is slack and full of differences, the tactic is to attack from three directions; as for the tactic against State Qin with increasing national power and strict laws and effective enforcement, the tactic is to lure with interest and attack while the soldier is unguarded; as for the plan toward State Chu with declining condition, broad land, disordered administration and sluggish people, the tactic is to attack its station to frustrate the morale and conduct a raid with cavalry to keep diminishing its confidence until the final victory.

Wu Qi also stands for the thought of attacking when the enemy is vulnerable, meaning to find out enemy's weakness first and confront with them when they are vulnerable. He listed eight typical predicaments, including marching under an extreme weather condition, in the shortage of army provisions and soldiers, delay of relief troops, and etc.

>《司马法》

《司马法》相传为司马穰苴所写，但到了战国时已经散失，现仅残存五篇，主要包括战争观、治军原则、军制、军令、军法、军礼和作战指导等方面内容，带有比较明显的儒家色彩。

《司马法》深受后人的推崇，在兵学界受到了极大的重视。汉武帝（前156年—前87）就依照《司马法》所定的标准来选任将领，北宋时《司马法》更成为培养军事人才的武学教材，是将校们的必读之书。

作者简介

司马穰苴，原名田穰苴，生卒年不详，春秋末期的军事家。他是

> Official Sima's Art of War

It's said that *Official Sima's Art of War* was written by Sima Rangju, which was missing by the Warring States Period (475 B.C.-221 B.C.) and only left five chapters, including the outlook on war, rules of military management, military system, military order, military courtesy and the command of the battle, with distinctive feature of the Confucian school.

Official Sima's Art of War has been praised highly by the later generations and also earned a great attention from other strategists. Emperor Wu of the Han Dynasty (156 B.C.-87 B.C.) selected all his military officers according to this book. In the Northern Song Dynasty (960-1127), this book even became the official textbook of martial arts.

• 司马穰苴（图片提供：FOTOE）
Portrait of Sima Rangju

齐国人，曾受到齐景公的重用，因军功被受任为大司马，故被后人称为司马穰苴。后来司马穰苴遭人陷害，被罢黜官职，不久抑郁而亡。

主要军事思想

在《司马法》中，“以仁为本”的经国治军理论也充分运用到了国家治理诸侯的过程中，如治理诸侯的六种办法：一是用调整封地的大小来控制诸侯，二是用政策法令约束诸侯，三是用财物说服诸

Biography

Sima Rangju, originally called Tian Rangju, unknown dates of birth and death, was a famous strategist in the late Spring and Autumn Period (770 B.C.-476 B.C.). Tian Rangju was from the State Qi and once appointed in significant position by King of Jing of the State Qi. Later he was assigned as the Great Sima (official position in charge of military affair), hence got the surname. Soon he was framed and dismissed from his position and died in depression.

Major Military Theory

In the book *Official Sima's Art of War*, the kindness oriented military management theory was applied to the national governance of vassals and derived six approaches: 1. control the vassals by adjusting the size of their feuds; 2. restrain them by administrative laws; 3. ingratiate them by gift or property; 4. assist them by resourceful man; 5. draw closer to them by rites or authority; 6. deter them with powerful military force. There are the methods avoiding to apply force, which reflects the kindness oriented thought.

Sima Rangju's military theory

春秋透雕龙纹戈

Hollowed Carved Dagger-axe (*Ge*) With Dragon Pattern (Spring and Autumn Period, 770 B.C.-476 B.C.)

侯，四是用有智谋的人去扶持诸侯，五是用礼仪威信亲近诸侯，六是用强大的军队慑服诸侯。这些做法均是避免使用武力的方法，充分体现了“以仁为本”的思想。

司马穰苴的治军理论侧重于军事教育，而不在于阐述技术和战术训练的具体内容。他提倡以仁、义、礼、智、信、勇来教育和培养军队，注重制定军法、军礼，强调赏罚分明。《司马法》为将领们提供了一些行之有效的治军方法：一是要有仁爱之心，二是要以诚相待，三是要以理服人，四是要有统一的要求，五是要做法得当，六是

focuses on the education of military affair instead of the detailed content of technique and tactical training. He advocated to apply benevolence, righteousness, manner, wisdom, faith and valiance to educate and nurture the army and paid attention to the establishment of military rules, courtesy and system of rewards and penalties. *Official Sima's Art of War* provides several practical and efficient management methods: the first is to keep the sympathy; the second is to treat others with sincerity; the third is to convince others by reasoning; the fourth is to set a uniform rules; the fifth is to act appropriately; the sixth is to handed with flexibility; the seventh is to concentrate

要灵活处置，七是要权力集中。如果将领能做到以上这几点，那么军队一定会秩序井然，战斗力也会大大提升。

此外，《司马法》还提出了“国容不入军，军容不入国”（朝廷的礼仪规章不能应用于军队，军队的法令也不能用于治国）的观点，告诫人们不能用治理军队的方法来治理国家，治国和治军有很大的区别。这是中国历史上第一次提

the power. If a military officer can hang on to these rules, then his army should be well-ordered and the combat effectiveness will be largely promoted.

Besides, *Official Sima's Art of War* also states a theory that the ritual system in the courtyard can not be applied in the army and vice versa. It alerts the people that there are enormous differences between the managements of a country and an army. It was the first time that the theory of separate

• 春秋铜剑
Bronze Swords (Spring and Autumn Period, 770 B.C.-476 B.C.)

出治国与治军应该分开的观点，具有极大的历史进步性，至今仍具有很大的借鉴意义。

春秋战国时期，诸侯争霸，干戈不断，是中国历史上的大变革时期。故此司马穰苴认为，虽然各诸侯国间应尽可能避免战争，但为了使当时的社会出现和谐的理想境界，必要的正义战争也是促进社会进步的重要手段，这便是他“以战

governance was mentioned, which was a historical development and still of great significance as a reference by now.

In the Spring and Autumn Period (770 B.C.-476 B.C.) and Warring States Period (475 B.C.-221 B.C.), when the vassals fell into endless conflicts and battles, it was a period of time with great revolution in Chinese history. Therefore, Sima Rangju thought although the vassals should try to avoid wars, yet with

• 春秋战国时期的战车

Chariot (Spring and Autumn Period and Warring States Period, 770 B.C.-221 B.C.)

止战”的战争观。《司马法》中提出：“杀人安人，杀之可也；攻其国爱其民，攻之可也；以战止战，虽战可也。”意思是，如果杀少数人是为了让更多人获得安宁，那么杀人是可以的；如果攻打一个国家是为了让这个国家的国民过更好的生活，那么攻打是可以的；如果发动战争的目的是为了制止战争，那么发动战争是可以的。《司马法》中还提出：“天下虽安，忘战必危。”意思是，如果一个国家长期没有战争，这并不表示和平，而恰恰预示着将要处于危险的境地。因此，国家要想长期生存下去的话，领导者一定要时刻保持着清醒的头脑，加强武备，这样在战争来袭时才能够从容应对，取得胜利。这种居安思危的国防观对后世有重大的指导意义。

the purpose of establishing a peaceful country, the inevitable war of justice could be the propelling power for the social development. And it is his famous theory of stopping the war with a war. In the *Official Sima's Art of War*, he stated: if killing people can make a peaceful world, then it can be tolerated; if taking a city and treating their people better, then the attack can be launched; to stop the war with a war, it is acceptable and reasonable. It means that if killing a few can get a peace for more people, then it can be tolerated; if attacking a state is in the purpose of giving them a better life, then the attack can be waged; if the purpose of the war is to get a peaceful world, then the war is inevitable. *Official Sima's Art of War* also states that if a state stays away from the war for a very long time, then it doesn't reflect the peace, yet a dangerous predicament of oncoming war. Therefore, if the state wants to survive for a long time, the leader should keep cautious and alert, and then it can deal with the battle calmly and seize the final victory. Such awareness of adversity is of great significance in guiding the theory of national defense of later generations.

秦灭齐之战

秦灭齐之战是"忘战必危"这一思想最好的印证。秦始皇二十六年（前221），秦军直逼齐都，俘虏了齐王，消灭了齐国，实现了中原的统一。齐国灭亡的主观原因就在于齐王长期不修武备，待秦军兵临城下时，只得束手就擒。

• **秦始皇蜡像**

秦始皇（前259—前210），姓嬴，名政，中国历史上第一个大一统王朝——大秦王朝的开国皇帝，被誉为"千古一帝"。

Wax Statue of Qin Shihuang

Qin Shihuang (259 B.C.-210 B.C.), named Yingzheng, was the first emperor of a united China in Chinese history and the founder of the Qin Dynasty (221 B.C.-206 B.C.), who is entitled as the First Emperor Through History.

Battle of Qin Conquering Qi

The battle of Qin conquering Qi is a good example of the theory of neglect leading danger. In 221 B.C., the Qin's army approached to the capital city of the State Qi, and captured the king of State Qi, which declared the collapse of the State Qi and the unification of the Central Plains in China. The doom of the State Qi was the result of the king's slack military management. When Qin's army was at the gate, the king can only fold his hands for capture.

• 秦始皇陵园内的士兵演练（模拟）
Military Drill in the Mausoleum of Qin Shihuang (Simulation)

>《孙膑兵法》

《孙膑兵法》又名《齐孙子》，约成书于战国中期，为孙膑及其弟子所著。《孙膑兵法》东汉以后就失传了，直到1972年，《孙

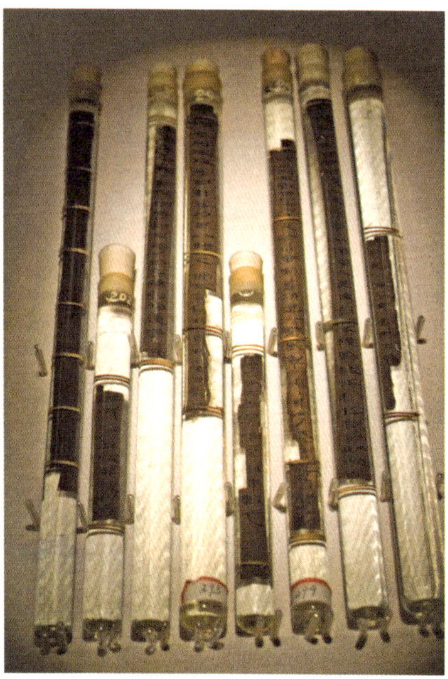

> Sun Bin's Art of War

Sun Bin's Art of War, also *Qi's Master Sun*, was approximately written in the middle of Warring States Period (475 B.C.-221 B.C.) by Sun Bin and his disciples. It was missing after the Eastern Han Dynasty (25-220) until 1972, the bamboo slips of *Sun Bin's Art of War* was excavated. The bamboo slips were badly damaged and could not be restored. After the clearing up by experts, it was proven to have 16 chapters. *Sun Bin's Art of War* has lots of development and innovation on the basis of carrying forward the

1972年山东临沂银雀山汉墓出土的《孙膑兵法》竹简（图片提供：FOTOE）

Bamboo Slips Excavated from the Tomb of the Han Dynasty on Yinque Mountain in Linyi City, Shandong Province

膑兵法》竹简才出土。出土时，竹简损坏十分严重，已不能恢复原貌，后经专家整理，编纂为《孙膑兵法》16篇。《孙膑兵法》在继承《孙子兵法》等前人兵法的基础上又多有发展和创新，且通篇充满了军事哲理，问世后受到了中外学者的普遍关注。

作者简介

孙膑，生卒年不详，战国中期的齐国人，杰出的军事家。孙膑在早年曾与庞涓一起学习兵法。庞涓学成后到了魏国，被魏惠王任命为

• 孙膑像
Portrait of Sun Bin

theory of *Master Sun's Art of War* and others' canons. It is filled with various military philosophies and has earned scholar's attention both at home and abroad.

Biography

Sun Bin, unknown dates of birth and death, from State Qi in the middle Warring States Period (475 B.C.-221 B.C.), was an outstanding strategist. In his early years, he once studied military theory with Pang Juan who went to State Wei and was appointed as general by King Hui of the Wei. Pang Juan knew clearly that he could not rival Sun Bin, so he lured Sun Bin to State Wei and applied *Bin* penalty (a cruel penalty in ancient China to remove the criminal's knee cap) to Sun Bin and pricked insulting words on Sun Bin's face with needle and ink. Later, the envoy from State Qi rescued Sun Bin and brought him back. He was recommended to King Wei of the Qi who extremely admired his talent and appointed him as the military counselor. Then, Sun Bin assisted the famous general Tian Ji of the State Qi to defeat Pang Juan twice and also won numerous battles, which laid the foundation for the rise of State Qi.

围魏救赵与马陵之战

公元前353年，魏国大军攻打赵国都城邯郸，赵王慌乱之中向齐国求救。齐国大将田忌和军师孙膑率军救赵。田忌采纳了孙膑“避实就虚”的策略，趁魏国都城兵力空虚，引兵直攻魏都。进攻赵都的魏军得到消息，只得班师回救。这时，齐军趁魏军疲惫，在他们返回的途中大败魏军，成功地解救了赵国。

公元前341年，魏军攻打齐国。孙膑在马陵道（今河南省范县）两侧埋伏了一万多名弓弩手。待夜幕降临，魏军首领庞涓率大队人马进入马陵道。齐军弓弩手万射齐发，大败魏军，庞涓自尽，此战共歼敌十万余人。

Relieve the State Zhao by Besieging the State Wei and the Battle of Maling

In 353 B.C., State Wei attacked the capital city of State Zhao, Handan. In the midst of panic, the king called State Qi for help. So general Tian Ji and military counselor Sun Bin

• 马陵之战

Battle of Maling

led a troop to rescue State Zhao. Tian Ji adopted Sun Bin's advice to avoid the main force and hit the weak point: he launched an attack to the capital city of State Wei directly while most of the soldiers were out to attack State Zhao. Wei's army got the message that their city was under attack, so they had to retreat and save their own capital city. While Wei's army was weary and halfway home, Qi's army launched a strike and defeated Wei's army and successfully saved State Zhao.

In 341 B.C., State Wei waged a war on State Qi. Sun Bin deployed about 10,000 crossbowmen along the two sides of Maling Path (today's Fan County, Henan Province). In the night, when Pang Juan, general of State Wei, led his army into Maling Path, crossbowmen shot arrows at the same time and defeated Wei's army. Pang Juan killed himself. And more than 100,000 soldiers were killed.

将军。庞涓自知才能不及孙膑，便把他骗到魏国加以陷害，对其施膑刑（去掉膝盖骨），并在脸上刺字涂墨。后来，齐国使者暗中将孙膑带回了齐国，推荐给齐威王。齐威王非常欣赏孙膑的才能，任其为军师。后来，孙膑辅佐齐国大将田忌两次击败庞涓，取得许多战争的胜利，奠定了齐国霸业的基础。

主要军事思想

《孙膑兵法》提出了“战胜而强立”的战争观。孙膑认为，国家只有取得了战争的胜利，才能够以

Major Military Theory

Sun Bin's Art of War, brought forward a concept of war: winner is stronger. Sun Bin believed that only when the country seizes the victory in the battle can it stand up as a powerful entity among others and can it keep moving on. He also mentioned the theory that if the importance of the war is neglected, then the country will end up in dead corner.

The concept that the winner is stronger was concluded by Sun Bin based on his deep analysis on the political situation at that time. According to the consecutive fights towards the hegemony among the vassals, he thought that

强者的姿态在社会中立足，才能够继续发展下去。他同时提出“乐兵者亡”，即忽视战争的重要性的国家，最终一定会灭亡。

“战胜而强立”的战争观是孙膑对当时的历史情形进行深入分析而得出的结论。他根据当时诸侯争霸的形势，列举了武王伐纣、周公东征等历史上的战争事例，说明人类社会自古以来就是用战争手段来实现统治目的的，企图用仁义、礼乐等办法消除战争、保存自己，那不过是一种不切实际的幻想。因此，各

people always achieve their political purpose through wars since antiquity. The intention to avoid wars and defend oneself from conflicts through righteousness, justice, manner and music was just an innocent fantasy. Therefore, the vassals could only establish a united country through wars and victories. So such concept of war satisfied the demand of getting united at that time, and had more positive significance than the theories raised by former strategist.

Sun Bin's Art of War states that the core of the theory of military management is to strengthen the army which is the base of the prosperity of the country. Sun Bin thought the victory of the fight among vassals depends on the solid material basis, developed economy

战国铜矛头

矛是中国古代重要的刺杀型兵器，也是古代军队中大量装备和使用时间最长的冷兵器之一。

Bronze Spearhead (Warring States Period, 475 B.C.-221 B.C.)

Spears are important stabbing weapon in ancient China, also one of the cold weapons which were largely equipped with the longest history.

诸侯国之间只有进行战争，并在战争中取得胜利，才能达到天下归一的目的。这种战争观适应了当时中国渐趋统一的客观形势需要，比前人的论述更具有切合时代的积极意义。

《孙膑兵法》治军思想的核心是“强兵”，而强兵的基础是“富国”。孙膑认为，要在群雄争霸中取得胜利，就要有雄厚的物质基础，不断发展经济，提高生产力，以此来建设强大的军队。在此基础上，良将和士卒是强兵的关键。强大的军队不仅要有善于部署阵战、灵活变换战法、掌握战争的主动权的良将，还要拥有经过严格选拔、

and advanced productivity to build a powerful army. And then, skillful and competent military officers and soldiers with high quality are the key. A powerful army needs not only excellent officers who can take the initiative of the battle with variant operation and deploy but also strictly trained soldiers who can abide by the disciplines and consequence management. A combination like this, can remain invincible in the war.

As to the operation theory, *Sun Bin's Art of War* emphasizes that one should follow the trend of the war and lead the war to the favorable direction. Sun Bin also raised series of principles to vanquish the enemy: if the home side

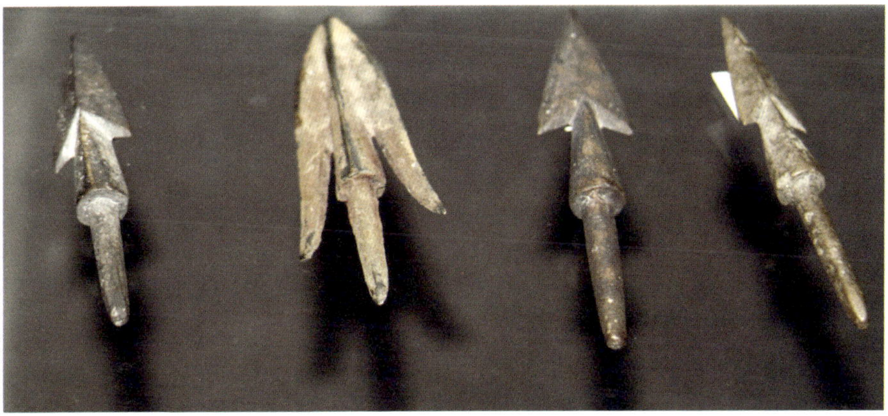

• 战国铜箭头
Bronze Arrowheads (Warring States Period, 475 B.C.-221 B.C.)

编制严密、令行禁止的士卒。这样的良将和士卒组成的强兵，才能够所向无敌。

在作战原则上，《孙膑兵法》强调“因其势而利导之”，即顺着战争发展的趋势，向有利于自己的方向加以引导。孙膑提出了一系列克敌制胜的原则：如在己强敌弱时要适当地示弱，藏起己方的优势，从而诱敌出战；敌强己弱时要先退一步，等到敌军疲乏时，再后发制人；势均力敌时要想办法迷惑、分散敌人，然后集中兵力，逐一击破；攻击走投无路的穷寇时要虚留生路，瓦解敌人的斗志，最终灭之。

is in advantage, then one should show the weakness and hide the advantage to lure the enemy out; if the home side is in disadvantage, one should take a step back and wait until the enemy shows the sign of fatigue and then gain mastery by later strike; if the home side ties with the enemy, one should find a way to confuse and distract the enemy and then focus all the force to hit them one by one; if attacking the desperate deserters, one should pretend to leave a way out and gradually break up their will and finally take them down.

巨鹿之战

巨鹿之战是在中国历史上发生的一次著名的以少胜多的战役。公元前207年，20万秦军包围赵国巨鹿（今河北平乡），赵王向楚国及各国诸侯求援。楚国的项羽主动请缨，率军六万余北上，以解巨鹿之困。在敌众我寡的情势下，项羽根据秦军兵力分散的布局，制定了相应的作战方案——各个击破。他先命部下率领两万人马进行试探性的进攻，多次袭击秦军运输粮草的甬道，打击秦军补给线，断其粮草，均取得胜利。在确认秦军少粮后，项羽意识到战机已到，亲率主力部队发起进攻。楚军只带了三天的干粮，抱着誓死决战的勇气与秦军展开了殊死决斗。项羽的军队作战勇猛，九战九捷，大获全胜，解除了巨鹿被围的危机。该战役是“因其势而利导之”的完美运用。

Battle of Julu

The Battle of Julu is a famous example of fighting against odds in Chinese history. In 207 B.C., Julu (today's Pingxiang County, Hebei Province) in State Zhao was besieged by Qin's army of 200,000 soldiers. The king of Zhao asked State Chu and other vassals for help. General Xiang Yu of State Chu volunteered for the rescue mission and led 60,000 soldiers towards the north. Under the disadvantage in the number, Xiang Yu planned an efficient tactic based on the scattered arrangement of Qin's army: to crush them one by one. At the beginning, he tried to organize tentative strikes with a 20,000 soldiers' troop and repetitively attack Qin's paved path for provision delivery to destroy their logistic support. Then, with the awareness of Qin's shortage of supply, Xiang Yu realized that it was the time. So he led the major force to attack Qin's army. As Chu's army (Xiang Yu) only brought the provisions for three days, so the soldier knew that it was a life-and-death battle and they all fought valiantly. Chu's army had a nine wins in a row and finally seized the victory of this war and secured Julu City. This battle is a perfect example for the theory of following the trend of the war and leading the war to the favorable direction.

• 巨鹿之战

Battle of Julu

>《六韬》

《六韬》大约成书于战国晚期，主要记述和反映了西周政治家姜太公的军事实践活动及军事思想，真实作者已不可考。全书共六卷六十篇，内容丰富，以周文王、周武王与姜太公对答的方式，详细论述了治国理军和作战指导的理论及方法，是先秦兵家的集大成之作，对后世产生了深远的影响。《六韬》有许多首创的内容，如记载了各种武器装备及其用途，反映了战国后期钢铁兵器大量用于装备军队的概况；记载了各种保密符牌和军情文书，反映了当时已经采用秘密手段传递军情的情况。

主要军事思想

治国有道一直是中国历代君主

> Six Strategies

Six Strategies, was completed in the late Warring States Period (475 B.C.-221 B.C.), mainly recording and reflecting the military practice and theory of a famous politics in the Western Zhou Dynasty (1046 B.C.-771 B.C.), Duke Jiang Taigong. The author is unknown to the world. This book has six volumes, sixty chapters, with rich content, which is narrated as conversation between King Wen and King Wu of the Zhou Dynasty and Duke Jiang Taigong. It states the theory and method of managing a country and an army as well as guiding principle of military operation in detail. It is a comprehensive expression of the strategists' theories before Qin Dynasty (221 B.C.-206 B.C.) and exerts profound influence on later generations. *Six Strategies* also includes many original contents, such as various weapons and

姜太公

姜太公，生卒年不详，又称吕尚、太公望，中国历史上著名的军事家、政治家和谋略家，先后辅佐了六位周王，并辅佐周武王灭商。商朝末年，纣王昏庸无道，诛杀忠良。姜太公身居深山研习兵法，应周文王之邀，助其兴周灭商。姜太公被誉为中国谋略家的开山鼻祖，其军事韬略在中国军事史上具有重要地位，对后世用兵起到了深远的影响。

Duke Jiang Taigong

Duke Jiang Taigong, unknown dates of birth and death, also named Lüshang, Taigong Wang, is a famous strategist, politician and tactician in Chinese history, who assisted six kings in the Zhou Dynasty and helped King Wu overturned the Shang Dynasty (1600 B.C.-1046 B.C.). In the late Shang Dynasty, the fatuous and tyrannical King Zhou killed many loyal and upright officials. At that time, Jiang Taigong who studied military tactic in mountains was invited by King Wen of the Zhou Dynasty to assist his ambitious cause. Duke Jiang Taigong has been praised as the patriarch of tactic. His theory plays an important role in Chinese military history and exerts a profound influence on the military management of later generations.

• 姜太公像

Portrait of Duke Jiang Taigong

们追求的目标，但到底何为治国之道，不同的君主有不同的看法。《六韬》中就为君主们提出了一个治国有道的方法——伐乱禁暴。《六韬》认为，只有德行高尚、善于治理国家的人才能君临天下。善于治理国家的君主，必须要施行仁政，对于拥护他的臣民要施与恩德，任其所能；对于作乱行暴的人，要进行讨伐。《六韬》还主张富国强兵，全力发展国家的农业、手工业和商业。让农民集中精力耕种土地，使粮食充足；让工人制造大量器物，使民众的器具充足；让

their functions, the facts that iron weapon largely equipped in army after the late Warring States Period (475 B.C.-221 B.C.), records about various confidential tokens and military documents, which reflect that the military intelligence had been delivered with confidential approach at that time.

Major Military Theory

The excellent governing principles have been pursued by all the kings and emperors in Chinese history. Yet, as to the definition of the governing principles, they have different opinions.

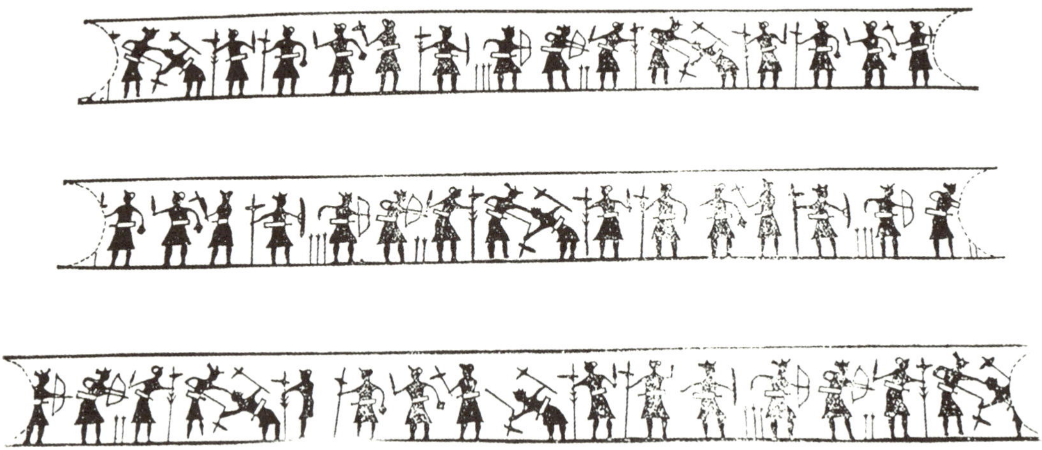

• 战国铜器纹饰中的攻战图
Battle Field Pattern on Bronze Vessel (Warring States Period, 475 B.C.-221 B.C.)

商人集中精力经营贸易，使货物供给通畅。这样才有足够的精力来制造兵器，保证战争的胜利。

"全胜"是《六韬》中想要达到的最佳的战争状态。"全胜"主要包含三个层次的含义：其一就是不通过战争，而是通过外交途径使别国顺从和归服，或者使用间谍等手法离间敌国的君臣，使其政治混乱，以达到不战而亡敌国的目的。其二是用强大的军事实力作为后盾，以大军压境的态势威慑敌国的君臣，瓦解敌军的斗志和士气。其三是指虽然出动军队，但是不通过战场上刀光剑影的兵戎相见，而是运用因敌而变的策略智取。总之就是要尽量做到不损一兵一卒，以最

Six Strategies provides an approach: against the riot and banning the tyranny. It says that only the moral and noble man who is good at national governance can ascend the throne. They should apply the policy of benevolence and show their kindness to the people who support their kingship and appoint the talent in accordance of their aptitude. As to the mobs who are against the authority, they should wipe them out. In the *Six Strategies*, it also stands for the policy of developing economy and enhancing the military power. The ruler should develop agriculture, handicraft industry and commercial trade: letting peasants concentrate on planting to get sufficient food, letting workers produce vessels to suffice people's demands, letting businessmen develop business to keep adequate supply. This way, the country can spend energy

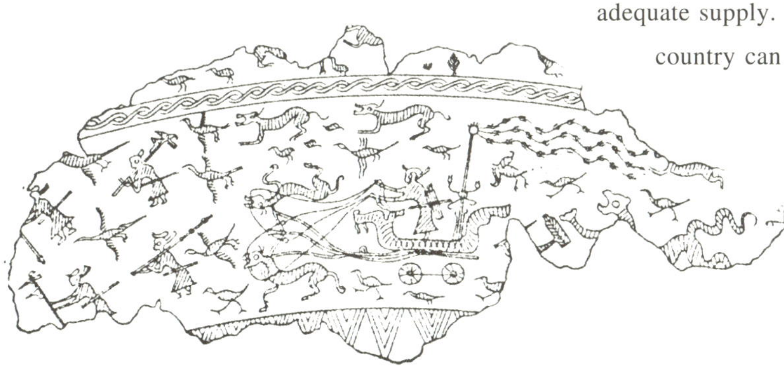

战国铜器纹饰中的行军图

Marching Pattern on Bronze Vessel (Warring States Period, 475 B.C.-221 B.C.)

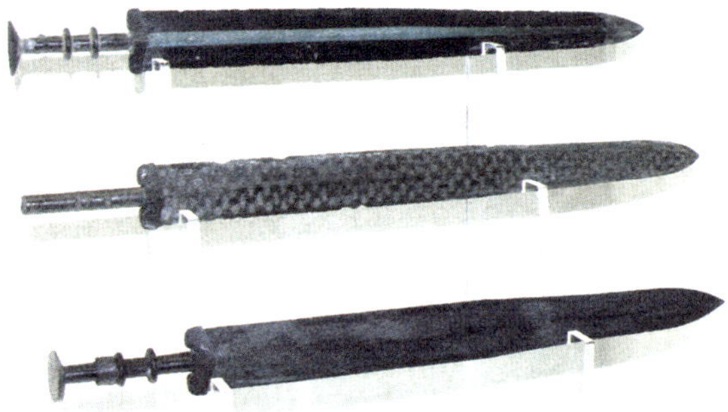

• 战国双色剑

春秋战国时期，铜剑制造业发达，制剑数量极大。早期铸剑的材料多为铜锡合金，锡硬且脆，铜较软但韧性好。古代工匠们在中心的剑脊采用含铜高的材料，保证了剑的韧性，剑刃则使用含锡较高的材料，保证了剑的锋利度。这种剑的剑脊颜色发黑，两刃发亮，剑身呈现两种颜色，故名“双色剑”。

Two-tone Swords (Warring States Period, 475 B.C.-221 B.C.)

In the Spring and Autumn Period (770 B.C.-476 B.C.) and Warring States Period (475 B.C.-221 B.C.), the bronze sword manufacturing industry was greatly developed. Numerous swords were produced at that time. The bronze sword in the early stage was made from copper-tin alloy, as tin is hard and fragile and copper is flexible. So ancient craftsmen used the material with high copper content to make the middle spine of the sword to guarantee its toughness and used the material with high tin content to make the blade to keep its sharpness. So this kind of sword will have a black spine and shiny blades, appearing with two colors, hence the name Two-tone Sword.

小的代价换取最大的胜利。

《六韬》将战争分为野战、攻城战、反攻战、突围战、追击战、伏击战、火攻等多种形式，并分别

and money to produce weapons in order to win the battles in the war.

The “complete victory” is considered as the best result of a battle in the book *Six Strategies*, which includes three meanings: the first is to bend other states through diplomatic approaches or to alienate the king and the officials of the enemy state through espionage activities to drag the opponent’s into chaos and attain the purpose of overturning the state without a war; the second is to use the powerful military force as its solid backing and to deter the enemy with imposing attacking troops to break the enemy’s fighting will and morale; the third is to depend on the tactic instead of direct conflict to defeat the enemy. In a word, the leader should avoid casualty and minimize the cost as much as possible.

Six Strategies states several types of battles, namely field operation, castle attack, counterattack, breakout, pursuit, ambush, fire attack, etc., and accordingly, gives different tactics. Moreover, *Six Strategies* also explains the tactics

给出了不同的战术方法。此外，《六韬》还论述了在森林、山地、河湖、要隘等特种地形作战的战术方法。

《六韬》十分重视对士兵的编组和训练，强调应从战争的实际需要来选拔和训练士兵，因人施教，因人而用。训练的重点首先是增强士兵的纪律性，然后再培训其战斗的技能。《六韬》中还对步兵、战车兵和骑兵这三大兵种的特点作了详细的比较，阐述了它们各自的优势和弱点，同时提出了协同作战的部署原则。

adopted in the forest, on the mountain, along the river or lake, in the strategic pass, etc.

Six Strategies emphasizes the organization and training of the soldiers. It stresses that the soldier should be selected and trained based on the actual need of the war and their own talent. The key point of the training is to enhance soldiers' sense of discipline and then teach them combat skills. Moreover, *Six Strategies* also makes a detailed comparison on the characteristics of infantry, chariot force and cavalry and states their advantages and disadvantages and also provides the deploy principle in the cooperative combat.

罚不避亲，赏不避过

唐朝开国皇帝李渊深受《六韬》治军论的影响，严明军纪，坚持做到“罚不避亲，赏不避过”（赏罚不考虑亲疏关系，不计较以往的过失），因而深受部属爱戴。

隋朝末年，天下混战，群雄割据。镇守太原的李渊趁机起兵，欲与群雄争夺天下。李渊招募贤才不分贫富贵贱，唯才是举，引得众人云集响应。在李渊的部队中，人们平等相待、和睦相处、团结一心。李渊曾当众宣布：“两军征战中，刀枪剑矢从不分贫富贵贱，因而奖励军功也应该一视同仁，论功行赏！”由于李渊坚持贯彻奖励军功一视同仁的政策，极大地鼓舞了士气，最终夺得了天下。

Punishing Without the Concern of the Close; Rewarding Without the Concern of the Guilty

The founder of the Tang Dynasty (618-907), Li Yuan was greatly inspired by the theories in the *Six Strategies*. He strictly abode by the discipline and sticked to the principle of Punishing Without the Concern of the Close; Rewarding Without the concern of the Guilty. Therefore he earned support and love from his people.

In the late Sui Dynasty (581-618), China was plunged into turmoil. Several warlords set up their own regime by force of arms. Li Yuan who guarded Taiyuan area led his army and joined the war. He recruited the talent regardless the social status or background which appreciated by many talented people. In his army, everybody was treated equally and lived as a united family. Li Yuan once declared that in the battle, the weapons have no differences from each other, so is the soldier. Everybody can get the equal chance to get the reward according to the achievement. Due to his consistent polity in rewarding, the soldier was greatly encouraged and finally helped him win the whole country.

• **唐高祖李渊像**

李渊（566—635），唐朝开国皇帝，中国杰出的政治家、战略家。

Portrait of Li Yuan, Emperor Gaozu of the Tang Dynasty

Li Yuan (566-635), the founder of the Tang Dynasty, was an outstanding politician and strategist in ancient China.

>《尉缭子》

《尉缭子》是一部系统的军事战略学著作，继承并发展了《孙子兵法》、《吴子兵法》等兵书的军事思想，受到中国乃至世界兵法研究者的推崇。该兵书成书于战国中后期，今存24篇，按内容可分为两部分：前12篇主要论述了作者的战争观和政治观，后12篇主要论述了军令和军制。《尉缭子》的军事理论以治国、富国为基础，对强兵、用兵的问题进行了广泛而深刻的研究。《尉缭子》是最早流传至国外的兵书之一，在日本、朝鲜和西方国家广为流传。该兵书的传播对于扩大中国古代军事文化的影响产生了重要的作用。

> *Wei Liao Zi*

Wei Liao Zi, a systematical canon on military strategies, which inherited and developed the theories in *Master Sun's Art of War* and *Master Wu's Art of War* has been praised by researchers of military strategy in China and even across the world. This book was written in the middle and late period of the Warring States Period (475 B.C.-221 B.C.), now existing 24 chapters. According to the content, it can be divided into two parts: the first half (1-12 chapters) is mainly about the concept of the war and politics and the second half (13-24 chapters) is mainly about the military disciplines and organization. The military theory in *Wei Liao Zi* is based on the national governance and development. It gives detailed research on the issues of military enhancement and operation. It was also

《武经七书》

《武经七书》是北宋朝廷颁行的官方兵法丛书，也是中国古代第一部军事教科书，用以考试和教学。这书由《孙子兵法》、《吴子兵法》、《六韬》、《司马法》、《三略》、《尉缭子》、《李卫公问对》汇编而成。《武经七书》集中了中国古代兵法的精华，被后世推崇为兵学经典，在中国军事史上具有重要影响。

Seven Military Canons

Seven Military Canons is a set of official military books issued by the authority of the Northern Song Dynasty (960-1127), also is the first set of military textbook in ancient China used for tests and teaching. It includes *Master Sun's Art of War, Master Wu's Art of War, Six Strategies, Official Sima's Art of War, Three Strategies, Wei Liao Zi,* and *Answers' Record of General Li Jing*, which covers all the essence in military strategy. It has been praised as a military classic by later generations and exerted great influence on Chinese military history.

作者简介

尉缭，生卒年不详，战国时期兵家。古人对所尊敬的人一般称“子”，故称其“尉缭子”。尉缭曾在魏国为臣，为振兴魏国付出了巨大努力，《尉缭子》一书就是他与魏王谈论军事学的记录。

主要军事思想

尉缭主张慎战，反对轻率用

one of the military books which were introduced to foreign countries, including Japan, Korea and the western countries. The spread of this book exerted a great influence on the expansion of ancient Chinese military culture.

Biography

Wei Liao, unknown dates of birth and death, was a military strategist in the Warring States Period (475 B.C.-221 B.C.). Ancient people liked to add

兵，但他支持正义的战争。他认为，“诛暴乱、禁不义”（平息暴乱、除掉不义）的战争是正义的，是不可避免的。

同时，尉缭认为经济是治国之本，是决定战争胜负的基础，政治清明是战争取胜的先决条件。这种把经济视为基础、把政治视为根本、把军事视为从属的见解在当时是难能可贵的。

尉缭总结出了三种夺取胜利的方式，即“以道胜”、“以威胜”、“以力胜”。“道”即方法和谋略，“威”即威势，“力”即兵力。其中，“以道胜”是用兵作战取胜的最高境界。要达到“以

• 战国越王勾践剑

Goujian, King of State Yue's Sword (Warring States Period, 475 B.C.-221 B.C.)

the character *Zi* behind the respected scholar's name, hence the name *Wei Liao Zi*. Wei Liao once served in the State Wei and contributed a lot for its prosperity. The book *Wei Liao Zi*, is the conversation record about military strategy between him and the king of the Wei.

Major Military Theory

Wei Liao stood for the cautious attitude towards war and was against the hasty attack, yet he agreed on launching the justice war and thought that the wars which can wipe out the riot and the injustice were inevitable and necessary.

Meanwhile, Wei Liao thought that the economy is the foundation of a country and also the key point that can greatly affect the result of the war, and an upright government is the prerequisite of the victory. His theory that sees economy as the foundation, the politics as the root and the military power as the collateral element was rare and insightful at that time.

Wei Liao concluded three winning approaches, namely winning through strategy, winning through deterrence and winning through force. Among the three, winning through strategy is the

岳飞收复六郡

南宋绍兴四年（1134），朝廷派大将岳飞率军收复被金朝掠夺的襄阳等六郡。在该战争中，岳飞灵活运用战略战术，诱敌深入，最终收复了六郡。此战是南宋抗金之战中的一次成功的大规模的反击战。可惜此时的皇帝却因宠信奸佞，没有采纳岳飞继续作战的建议，丧失了抗金的最佳战机，终致功亏一篑。可见，“兵胜于朝廷”，政治清明是战争取胜的先决条件。

Yue Fei's Retrieving Six Counties

In 1134, the general Yue Fei was appointed to retrieve the six counties (including Xiangyang, etc.) occupied by the Jin Dynasty (1115-1234). In this war, he applied various tactics to lure the enemy into the trap and finally retrieved the six counties. This was a successful counterattack operation in the Southern Song Dynasty (1127-1279). Unfortunately, the emperor favored and trusted the treacherous official and didn't accept Yue Fei's advice for further expansion and missed the best opportunity to overturn the Jin Dynasty. Clearly, an upright government is the prerequisite of the victory in the war.

• 岳飞杀敌
Yue Fei in Combat

道胜”，将帅的才能就显得尤为关键。尉缭认为“上不制于天，下不制于地，中不制于人”是将帅所需具备的武德（意思是将帅必须上不受到天时的限制，下不受到地形的限制，中不受到人为的限制，这才算是一个优秀的将帅）。在具体的战术上，尉缭提出了许多先进的方法，例如士兵在列阵时，可“有内向，有外向，有立阵，有坐阵”，即有人朝向内，有人朝向外，有人

best result. In order to attain this, the talent of the officials appears to be the key point. In Wei Liao's opinion, he thought the leader should not be affected by weather, climate, terrain, and people. As to the specific tactics, Wei Liao raised many advanced methods. For example, when soldiers arrange the array, they should perform in different gestures like standing, sitting or kneeling as well as facing different directions to keep flexible and motivated. The Terracotta Warriors

• 春秋战国时期的步兵方阵

Square Array of Infantry (Spring and Autumn Period and Warring States Period, 770 B.C.-221 B.C.)

• 战国末期的士兵装束
Military Uniform (Warring States Period, 475 B.C.-221 B.C.)

采取站姿，有人采取坐姿或跪姿。这种阵法错落有致，十分灵活，方便指挥，秦始皇陵中的兵马俑就有按这种阵法排列的。

在《尉缭子》中，作者还明确指出了法制建设的重要性。尉缭认为，法制不但是治国的根本，也是治军的根本。任何一支军队，只有先制定系统而严明的制度，官兵的作战训练才能有秩序地进行，在作战时也才能号令明确、行动统一、所向披靡。

in Qin Shihuang's Mausoleum also adopted such array.

In the book Wei Liao Zi, it also raises the importance of legal construction. Wei Liao thought that the legal construction is not only the foundation of the country, also the base of military management. The army can only carry out regular training with strict rules and disciplines. And the order can be carried out consistently in the battle to keep itself invincible in the battle.

>《三略》

《三略》是一部兼采众家之长而又自成体系的军事理论著作，也是中国第一部以政治策略和军事战略的关系为论述重点的兵书。《三略》约成书于西汉末年（一说东汉末年），全书分上、中、下三卷。

相较于《孙子兵法》、《孙膑兵法》、《六韬》等兵书，《三略》更侧重于政治战略的论述，主要从治国强国的角度出发，探讨取胜的政治谋略。此外，该兵书还引用了许多古代军事谚语，来表达作者的思想观点。

作者简介

《三略》的作者不详，据史学家推测可能是汉代一位精通兵法的

> Three Strategies

Three Strategies is a military canon referring to all the strong points raised by other strategists and also having its own theoretical system. It is also the first military book focusing on the relationship between political and military tactics. It was written around the late Western Han Dynasty (206 B.C.-25 A.D.) (or late Eastern Han Dynasty, 25-220), with three volumes.

Comparing with *Master Sun's Art of War*, *Sun Bin's Art of War*, and *Six Strategies*, *Three Strategies* lays particular emphasis on the explanation of political tactics. It is mainly from the perspective of national governance and economic development to discuss the winning strategy. Moreover, this book also quotes many military proverbs and idioms to support the author's opinion.

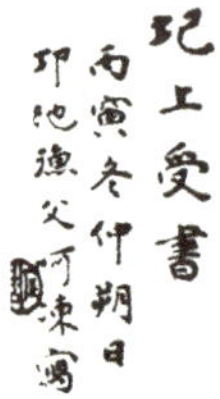

《圯上受书》（图片提供：FOTOE）

此画为清末民初马骀所作，描绘了黄石公授予张良兵法的故事。

Giving Book on the Bridge

This painting was drawn by Ma Tai in the late Qing Dynasty (1644-1911), which depicts the story of Huang Shi giving Zhang Liang the military book.

隐士。民间传说《三略》为秦末汉初的隐士黄石公所著，故《三略》又称《黄石公三略》。在《史记》中还记载了黄石公授张良兵书的故事。相传秦朝末年，张良有一天路过一座桥时，一位老翁故意将鞋甩到桥下让张良去捡。张良恭敬地将鞋捡起，并给老翁穿上。后来，老翁便送了一本书给张良，并对他说："你读了这本书就可以做帝王

Biography

According to the speculation of the historian, *Three Strategies* might be written by a hermit in the Han Dynasty (206 B.C.-220 A.D.) who excelled in military strategy. Legend has that, it was written by the old man Huang Shi. So it was also called *Huang Shi's Three Strategies*. In the *Historical Records*, it records the story about Huang Shi teaching Zhang Liang military tactics. It says that in the late Qin Dynasty, a young man named Zhang Liang walked by a bridge. An old man threw his shoe under the bridge on purpose and asked Zhang Liang to bring the shoe back. Zhang Liang helped him with respect and put it on the old man's foot. Afterwards, the old man gave Zhang Liang a book and told him, "If you can go through this book, then you can build an army which can conquer the world." This old man was Huang Shi and the book was *Three*

之师了。”这位老翁就是黄石公，而这本书就是《三略》。若干年后，张良果真辅佐刘邦开创了西汉王朝。

Strategies. Several years later, Zhang Liang assisted Liu Bang to establish the Western Han Dynasty.

主要军事思想

民本思想千百年来一直影响着中国人民，而这种思想也被《三略》所借鉴。《三略》从民本思想出发，对安国、选将、治军、作战等一系列问题进行了深入的论述。《三略》认为，战争的胜败在于国家治理的好坏，而民心的向背又是国家治理得好坏的关键。如果国家

Major Military Theory

People-oriented thought has been influenced Chinese people for thousands of years, which has been referred in the book *Three Strategies*. *Three Strategies* is based on the people-oriented thought and develops in-depth discussion on national security, talent selection, military management and battle operation. *Three Strategies* states that the result of the war depends on the situation of the national governance

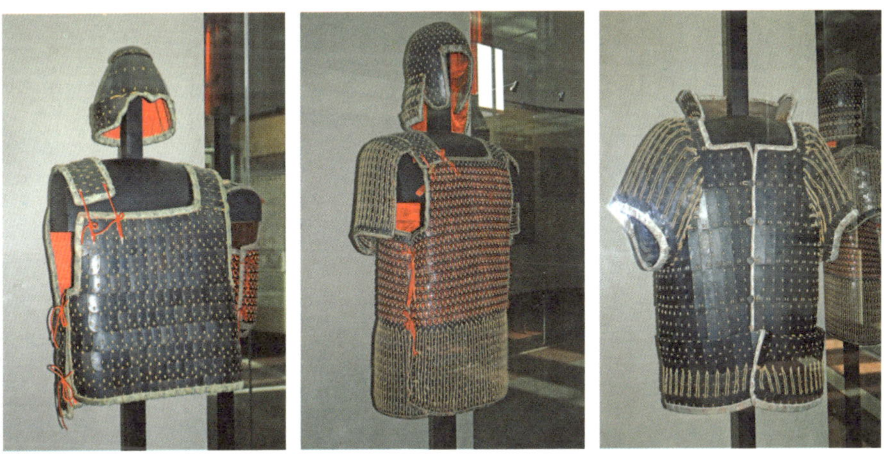

• 汉代甲胄

Armors (Han Dynasty, 206 B.C.-220 A.D.)

得到民众的拥护，国家就会安定，军队就能壮大，兵锋所向，就无往不胜；如果国家治理得不好，国虚民贫，民众被迫反抗，如果敌人趁机来犯，国家就会崩溃。因此，无论是治理国家还是统兵作战，都要随时随地“察民心，施民务”。

《三略》在治军问题上，既重视将帅的指挥作用，又重视士兵的战斗作用。认为将帅是统率全军、创造有利态势、战胜敌人的指挥

which is mostly determined by the will of the people. If the authority is supported by the public, the nation will be stable and the army will be strengthened and become invincible. If the government is in bad shape, the country is weak and the people are in misery. The enemy might take the advantage and launch an attack while the country is in the turmoil, which will directly lead to the doom of the government. Therefore, whether the national governance or the military operation, the leader should carefully observe the public opinion and satisfy people's need.

Regarding to the military management, *Three Strategies* emphasizes not only the command of the officer but also the fighting capacity of the soldier. He thought the officer is the leader who can create advantage for the army

汉代骑兵塑像

Statue of Han Cavalry

• 汉代步兵装束

Military Uniform of Infantry (Han Dynasty, 206 B.C.-220 A.D.)

者，士兵则是奋勇战斗、消灭敌人的主力。因此，将帅既要有优良的品德和广博的知识，又要做到清廉、镇静、公平、恩威并重、赏罚分明。

《三略》还集中讨论了国家如何才能用最明智的方法取得战争胜利。如“释远谋近”，即放弃远的国家而攻打近的国家，这样就可以较容易地取得成功。因为攻打远方的国家会使自己的军队过于劳累而失去斗志，而如果暂时放弃远方

and then to defeat the enemy. And the soldier is the main force to eliminate the enemy. Therefore, the officer should be moral and knowledgeable, as well as upright and calm, with sense of justice. He should employ both kindness and severity and keep the rewarding and punishment fair and convincing.

Three Strategies also discusses the strategies of winning the war with the most sensible approach, such as abandon the distant and attack the close, meaning to give up the state far from itself and choose to attack the close state. In this way, one can easily achieve the victory. Because, attacking the distant state will make the army too exhausted and lose the will of fight. If one can abandon the distant state and try to conquer the close states through tactics. It can largely

的国家，使用策略去降服近旁的国家，这样不仅壮大了自己的实力，还能避免劳民伤财，得到百姓的爱戴，最终一定能建立霸业。

expand the state's own power and also avoid waste of manpower and money, which will earn him the public support and finally lead him to the throne.

• 汉代楼船（模型）

楼船是中国古代水面战场上的主力作战舰只，由多层建筑和攻防设施组成。

Towered Ship in the Han Dynasty(Model)

The towered ship is the major warship in ancient water battle in China, which is composed by the structures with multiple storeys and equipment used for attack and defense.

>《三十六计》

《三十六计》是集历代韬略、诡道之大成的一部通俗易懂的兵书。该书分为两大部分，一部分是以优胜劣的作战计谋，包括“胜战计”、“敌战计”、“攻战计”三套；另一部分是以劣胜优的作战计谋，包括“混战计”、“并战计”、“败战计”三套。每一套计谋各又分为六计，共三十六计。《三十六计》中，每一计都是众所周知的成语，易记易理解，因此能在群众中广为流传。《三十六计》中所蕴含的道理是对于中国古代社会政治、经济、军事等活动的规律与方法的集中分析阐释，在当今社会的各个领域也得到了广泛的应用。

> Thirty-Six Stratagems

Thirty-Six Stratagems, is a popular strategic book which includes all the tactics and schemes raised by former masters. It has two parts: one is about the tactics for the advantaged side, including winning tactic, enemy tactic and attack tactic (total three sets); the other is about the tactics for the disadvantaged side, including wild tactic, joint tactic and defeat tactic (total three sets). And each set also includes six stratagems, totally 36 stratagems. In the book, each stratagem is written in popular idiom, which is convenient to remember and understand. Therefore, it can be widely spread among the people. The theories implied in the *Thirty-Six Stratagems* explain the rules and principles of the social politics, economy and military activity in ancient China, which are still broadly applied in various domains nowadays.

三十六计 Thirty-Six Stratagems	以优胜劣 For the Advantaged Side	胜战计 Winning Tactic	瞒天过海、围魏救赵、借刀杀人、以逸待劳、趁火打劫、声东击西 cross the sea by a trick; relieve the State Zhao by besieging the State Wei; borrow a knife to kill a man; wait at one's ease for an exhausted enemy; loot a burning house; look one way and row another
		敌战计 Enemy Tactic	无中生有、暗度陈仓、隔岸观火、笑里藏刀、李代桃僵、顺手牵羊 create something out of nothing; attack Chencang while drawing enemy's attention to the plank road; look on the fire with indifference; hide a dagger behind a smile; sacrificing the plum tree for the peach tree; pick up sheep on the sly
		攻战计 Attack Tactic	打草惊蛇、借尸还魂、调虎离山、欲擒故纵、抛砖引玉、擒贼擒王 act rashly and alert the enemy; revive in a new guise; lure the enemy away from his base; leave somebody at large the better to apprehend him; throw out a minnow to catch a whale; defeat the enemy by capturing their leader
	以劣胜优 For the Disadvantaged Side	混战计 Wild Tactic	釜底抽薪、浑水摸鱼、金蝉脱壳、关门捉贼、远交近攻、假道伐虢 pull out the firewood under the cauldron; make a profit in troubled situation; escape by crafty scheme; catch the thief by closing his escape route; associate with the distant countries and attack the near ones; attack the enemy by passing through a common neighbor
		并战计 Joint Tactic	偷梁换柱、指桑骂槐、假痴不癫、上屋抽梯、树上开花、反客为主 replace the major force under the disguise; point at one but abuse another; feign madness without being insane; lure the enemy into the trap; put fake flower on the trees to pretend the blooming prosperity; turn from the defense into the attack
		败战计 Defeat Tactic	美人计、空城计、反间计、苦肉计、连环计、走为上 honey-trap; empty city tactic; counter-spy tactic; self-injury tactic; interlocking stratagems; walking away is the best choice

作者简介

《三十六计》究竟为何人所著、何年撰写，至今尚未有定论，但有不少学者认为该书为南北朝时期檀道济所著，明清之际流传开来。檀道济（？—436），南朝著名将领，戎马一生，智勇兼备，战绩卓著。

主要军事思想

《三十六计》强调，善于用兵的人，一定要避开敌军旺盛的士气，不采取直接进攻的战略，而是

• 檀道济像
Portrait of Tan Daoji

Biography

The author and exact finishing time of the book *Thirty-Six Stratagems* haven't confirmed yet. Many scholars assume this book was written by Tan Daoji in the Southern and Northern dynasties (420-589) and was widely spread in the Ming Dynasty (1368-1644) and Qing Dynasty (1644-1911). Tan Daoji (?-436), was a famous general in the Southern Dynasties, who dedicated his whole life to protect his country. He was brave and also very resourceful, which helped him achieve several great accomplishments.

Major Military Theory

Thirty-Six Stratagems emphasizes that the man who excels in military operation knows to avoid the enemy with high morale and defense the position instead of the direct attack to consume the enemy's fighting will. While the opponent becomes exhausted, then launch a strike. Meanwhile, the local stationed soldier can be selected to attack the hostile army who comes from distant place. The rested soldiers can be selected to confront with the exhausted enemy. The satiated soldiers can be selected to deal with the hungry enemy. These are

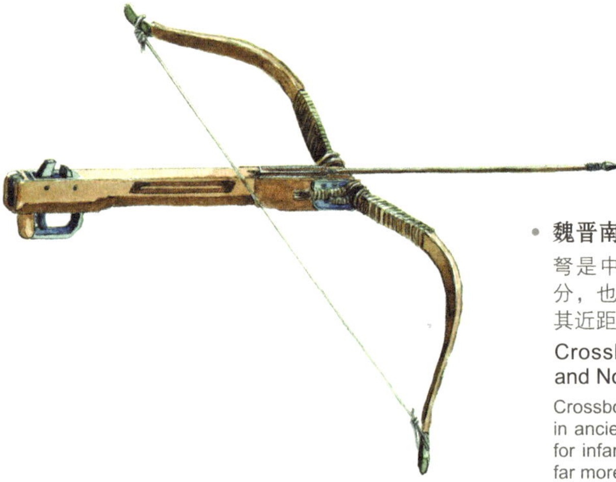

- **魏晋南北朝时期的弩**

弩是中国古代兵车战法中的重要组成部分，也是步兵有效克制骑兵的一种武器，其近距离的杀伤力远大于弓。

Crossbow (Wei, Jin and the Southern and Northern dynasties, 220-589)

Crossbow is an important part of chariot tactic in ancient China, and also an efficient weapon for infantry whose lethality in close distance is far more powerful than the bow.

- **魏晋南北朝时期的水战场景**

Water Battle (Wei, Jin and the Southern and Northern Dynasties, 220-589)

夷陵之战

公元221年7月，为争夺战略要地荆州，刘备率领10万蜀军向东吴发动进攻，孙权命陆逊率领五万吴军迎战。

陆逊根据对两军兵力、地形等诸多因素的准确分析，决定以逸待劳，主动撤军，退守夷陵、猇亭（今湖北宜都市北）一线，并部署防线，等待战机。刘备率领主力军队驻军猇亭，连营数百里。为引诱吴军出兵，刘备采取了围攻、阵前辱骂、山地设伏等多种计谋，但陆逊均拒不出战，彻底瓦解了刘备倚仗优势兵力速战速决的战略意图。两军相持数月，蜀军斗志涣散、士气低落。陆逊见进攻时机成熟，同时了解到蜀军军营密集，营地周围都是易

陆逊火攻蜀营

Fire Attack on Shu's Camp Conducted by Lu Xun

燃之物，便采取火攻，夜袭蜀营，同时派兵攻击蜀军前部和两翼，切断了蜀军的退路。蜀军慌忙迎战，无法组织有效反抗，纷纷逃散，死伤无数。刘备见大势已去，败走马鞍山（夷陵西的长江南岸）。夷陵之战是“以逸待劳”思想的成功运用，也是三国时期具有决定性意义的一次大战。

Battle of Yiling

In the July of 221, the State Wu and State Shu were fighting for a strategic area, Jingzhou. Liu Bei, leader of the State Shu led 100,000 soldiers to attack the State Wu. On the other hand, leader of the State Wu, Sun Quan appointed general Lu Xun to lead 50,000 soldiers resist the strike.

According to the analysis on the military power, terrain and other elements, Lu Xun waited at his ease for the exhausted enemy and retreat to Yiling and Xiaoting (today's Yidu City, Hubei Province) on purpose to arrange the defense line and wait for opportunity. Liu Bei stationed his army at Xiaoting stretching for hundreds of kilometers. In order to lure Wu's army out, Liu Bei applied several tactics like siege, insult and mountain ambush. However, Lu Xun refused to come out, which completely sabotaged Liu Bei tactic intention to fight a quick battle relying on his advantage in the number of the soldiers. After several months, Shu's army lost their morale. Then Lu Xun saw the opportunity and launched a fire attack at night since he knew that Shu's camps were built closely among many inflammable materials. Meanwhile, he sent troops to attack the enemy's forehead and flanks and cut off their retreat path. In a panic, Shu's army was forced to confront with Wu's attack. They couldn't organize efficient defense and most of them were killed or escaped. Liu Bei saw the failure and escaped to Ma'anshan (today's southern bank of the Yangtze River in the west of the Yiling). This battle is an excellent example for the theory of waiting at one's ease for an exhausted enemy, also a significant battle in the Three Kingdoms Period (220-280).

坚守阵地，消磨敌军的士气，使敌军势力损耗，当敌军疲于奔命时再出击。同时，将领应选用一直驻守此地的士兵来攻打远道而来的敌军，用休整完好的士兵来攻打疲惫不堪的敌军，用饱食的士兵来攻打饥饿的敌军，这才是从实力上战胜敌人的最好方法。这便是胜战计中的“以逸待劳”。

攻战计中的“欲擒故纵”，是强调将领在战争中要保持良好的作战心态，不要过于焦虑和急躁。如果攻击敌军过于猛烈，反倒可能会被敌人反扑，这是军之大忌。而如果换一种方式，如选择让敌人逃跑，就会削弱敌人的士气，这时再紧紧地追击

the good methods to triumph over the enemy, which are referred in the winning tactic as “waiting at one’s ease for an exhausted enemy”.

The stratagem of “leaving somebody at large the better to apprehend him” in the attack tactic emphasizes that the leader should maintain a good mental condition in the battle and avoid the anxiety and irritation. Forcing the enemy to the corner might cause more violent counterattack, which is a taboo in military operation. On the contrary, letting the enemy escape might eliminate enemy’s morale. At this time, one can chase them out of the map until the enemy loses its fighting capacity. Then there only leaves weak and scattered soldiers waiting to be captured. The victory is also at fingertips.

In the *Thirty-Six Stratagems*, it says “Thirty-six stratagems, walking away is the best choice”,

魏晋南北朝时期执盾的武士陶俑

Clay Statue of a Warrior Carrying a Shield (Wei, Jin, Southern and Northern Dynasties, 220-589)

• 南北朝时期的作战场景

Battle Field (Southern and Northern Dynasties, 420-589)

敌人，等到敌军体力衰竭、斗志全无、兵力分散时再去擒拿敌军，便可轻松取得战争的胜利。

《三十六计》有云：“三十六计，走为上。”这句话在中国妇孺皆知。这里的“走”，并非指逃跑，而是机动行军、迂回作战、以退为进之意。这就是说，如果作战双方的军事实力过于悬殊，完全没有战胜敌军的可能，那么将领就要及时撤兵或迂回作战，保存实力，以便在不利的态势中寻求有利态势，在被动中争取主动，转败为胜。

which is widely known by almost all the Chinese. The word “walking away” here means flexible defense, taking a detour and retreating for another attack instead of the pure escape. In other words, if the military power of both sides is very unbalanced, and there is no chance to resist the enemy, then the leader should retreat or take a detour to save the strength for further favorable possibility in case in disadvantage. It can help the passive side turn the table and find the chance to win the war.

四川宜宾"三十六计"摩崖石刻（图片提供：FOTOE）

The Inscriptions on Precipices of Thirty-Six Stratagems in Sichuan Yibin

>《李卫公问对》

《李卫公问对》，又称《唐太宗李卫公问对》，以唐太宗李世民与将领李靖论兵的问答形式辑录成书，由李靖编撰。全书共提出和回答了98个问题，对前人的军事思想进行了正面的评论和扬弃，对军制、阵法、选将练兵、军事教育、边防建设等问题进行了论述，并引用了52个典型的战例加以论证。可以说，《李卫公问对》对中国军事理论的发展起到了承前启后的作用。

作者简介

李靖（571—649），唐朝的著名将领、军事家，封卫国公，精通文史，自幼熟读《孙子兵法》。在李靖的戎马生涯中，所指挥的几次

> Answers' Record of General Li Jing

Answers' Record of General Li Jing, also called *Answers' Record of General Li Jing Discussing with Emperor Taizong*, is a collection of the conversation about military issues between Emperor Taizong of the Tang Dynasty (618-907), Li Shimin and his general Li Jing. It was compiled by Li Jing, including total 98 questions and answers which give direct comments on former military theories and principles and discuss the issues about military organization, array, officer selection and military training, military education and frontier construction. It also quotes 52 typical examples to support the arguments. Therefore, this book serves as a transitional bridge for the development of the military theory in China.

• 李靖像
Portrait of Li Jing

重大战役都取得了胜利，帮助唐太宗平定天下、开疆扩土。李靖根据自己的实战经验，著有数种兵书，但大多已亡佚。

主要军事思想

“奇正” 是中国古代的军事术语。狭义的奇正是以对阵交锋为正，设伏掩袭等为奇。而广义的奇正既被用于解释政治和军事等领域中出现的矛盾对立统一的范畴，又指哲学领域中矛盾对立统一的关

Biography

Li Jing (571-649), a famous general, strategist, entitled as the Duke of State Wei, excelled in history and started to study *Master Sun's Art of War* in his early ages. In his military life, he won several important battles, which greatly contributed to Emperor Taizong's cause. Li Jing wrote various military books based on his own experience. However, most of them were lost.

Major Military Theory

Surprising and Traditional are military terms in ancient China. In narrow sense, the Traditional indicates the direct combat and the Surprising indicates ambush and raid. However, generally, these terms can not only explain the contradictory in politics and military activities, also in philosophy. In *Answers' Record of General Li Jing*, the discussion about Surprising and Traditional is complete and incisive. It explains that Surprising is tactic, meaning in the battle, the leader should use tactic to guide the operation; and Traditional is integrity, meaning the leader should use moral bound and legal system to govern the country. Li Jing applied the Surprising and Traditional

唐太宗李世民

唐太宗李世民（599—649）是唐代的第二代皇帝。他雄才大略，智勇双全，精于兵法，善于在战争中使用出奇制胜的战法，并且在作战时能身先士卒。在位期间，他选贤任能，虚心纳谏，文治武功均有建树，开创了封建社会的盛世——“贞观之治”。唐太宗选贤任能的美德和对于兵法的精通在《李卫公问对》这本兵书中均有体现。

Emperor Taizong, Li Shimin

Emperor Taizong, Li Shimin (599-649), was the second emperor in the Tang Dynasty (618-907), who was very talented and also valiant. He excelled in military strategy and was able to perform surprising tactic in the battle. He also led the army by himself and fought with his soldiers. In his reign, he selected the talent and accepted others' opinions with an open mind. He achieved great accomplishment both in the national governance and military expanse. He created a flourishing age in feudal society: Age of Zhenguan. Li Shimin's virtue and talent are all reflected in the book *Answers' Record of General Li Jing*.

• 唐太宗李世民像
Portrait of Emperor Taizong, Li Shimin

系。在《李卫公问对》中，关于奇正的论述完备而精辟，认为奇即“奇道”，是说打仗时要用谋略指挥军队作战；正即“正道”，是说治理国家要通过道德和法律的手

in the military activities and he believed their variants are endless and so are the ways getting the victory. So the leader should fully observe the situation and find out the winning factors.

• 唐代骑兵
Cavalries (Tang Dynasty, 618-907)

段。李靖将奇正的方法灵活应用于战争中，认为奇正的变化是无穷无尽的，取胜的方法是多种多样的，应该全面考察和研究影响战争胜负的因素。

“致人而不致于人”的思想始于《孙子兵法》，体现了作战指挥时要争取主动权的思想。李靖十分推崇这一思想，并在《李卫公问对》中进行了发展和创新。李靖指

The theory of "holding the enemy instead of being held" was originated from *Master Sun's Art of War*, reflecting the idea that one should take the initiative in the battle. Li Jing praised highly about this theory and developed it in the book *Answers' Record of General Li Jing*. Li Jing pointed out that either the attack or the defense needs to seizes the initiative and compare the fighting capacity to turn the disadvantages into favorable

出，无论是进攻还是防御，都需要掌握主动权，比较敌我双方的强弱态势，将我方的不利态势转化为有利态势。进攻时，应先分析敌人的企图，摧毁敌人的斗志。防御时，应避敌锋芒，最大限度地挫败敌军锐气，养精蓄锐，待敌军实力削弱时再进行反击。

此外，李靖认为通过各种方法保存军队的战斗力是取得战争胜利的一个重要因素，并提出了六种可

condition. In the attack, the leader should analyze enemy's intention and destroy their fighting will; in the defense, the leader should avoid the main force and try to break their momentum, save the energy and wait until the enemy shows its weakness, and then launch the counter attack.

Moreover, Li Jing believed that preserving the combat capacity is a crucial factor for winning the battle and he raised six methods to save the energy:

唐代战争场景

Battle Field (Tang Dynasty, 618-907)

平萧铣之战

公元621年，为了争夺江南地区的控制权，唐朝大将李靖率军与江陵萧铣政权在长江流域交战。适逢雨季，江水暴涨，萧铣认为唐军必因道路行阻不能准时发兵，于是命令士兵休整。但李靖却派遣战舰2000余艘按期出兵，打得萧铣措手不及。于是萧铣部队仓促发起进攻，李靖领兵迎战，斩杀敌军近万人，虏获舟船400余艘。李靖又趁势率领5000人的先头部队围困江陵，杀伤、俘虏敌军4000余，缴获数千艘舟船。为动摇敌军军心，李靖还将俘获的战船推入江中。前来救援萧铣的将领赶到后，看到江中战船散乱漂下，以为江陵已被唐军攻破，不敢继续前进。孤立无援的萧铣屡战屡败，只得出城投降。

Battle Against Xiao Xian's Authority

In 621, in order to seize the control in the southern areas of the Yangtze River, general Li Jing led army to confront with Xiao Xian's Authority at the area of the Yangtze River.

- **唐代骑兵蜡像**

  Wax Statues of Tang Cavalries

While it was rainy season, the river water rose suddenly and sharply. Xiao Xian assumed that Tang's army should be delayed due to the road block. So he ordered the soldiers to have a rest. However, Li Jing knew that speed is too important in the war. So he sent more than 2,000 warships as planned and attacked Xiao Xian without preparation. So Xiao Xian's army launched the war hastily. Li Jing went out to fight, who killed almost 10,000 soldiers and captured more than 400 warships. Moreover, Li Jing took the advantage and led 5,000 soldiers to besiege the Jiangling City, killed and captured more than 4,000 enemy's soldiers and thousands of boats. In order to deter the enemy, Li Jing ordered to push the captured boats into the river. When the relief troops arrived, they saw the sinking boats and thought Jiangling had been taken by Tang's army. So they wouldn't step forward. Soon, without the help, Xiao Xian was force to go out and surrendered to the Tang's army.

以保存军队战斗力的方法：在战争中要始终保持沉着稳重，缺乏全面考虑而轻举妄动常常会失败；在备战时也要时刻严阵以待，等待敌人的军队懈怠松弛时便可发兵；以假象来诱惑敌人，等待敌人落入陷阱；在防御时要冷静、耐心，等待敌人急躁冒进的发兵；在敌人进攻之前，一定要尽全力对军队进行部署；一定要确保军队井然有序，切不可杂乱无章就发兵。

《李卫公问对》中非常重视军队的管理、教育和训练，提出"教得其道"，即军队的教育要遵循一

in the war, one should keep calm and prudent, lacking of consideration usually leads to the failure; in the preparation, one should keep the army alert and wait for enemy's sluggish moment to attack; one can lure the enemy with false alarm and wait for them falling into the trap; in the defense, one should remain calm and patient, and wait for the opponent rushing through; before the attack, one should carefully arrange the deploy; one should make sure the army will abide by the disciplines. Do not send the army without disciplines.

Answers' Record of General Li Jing emphasizes the military management,

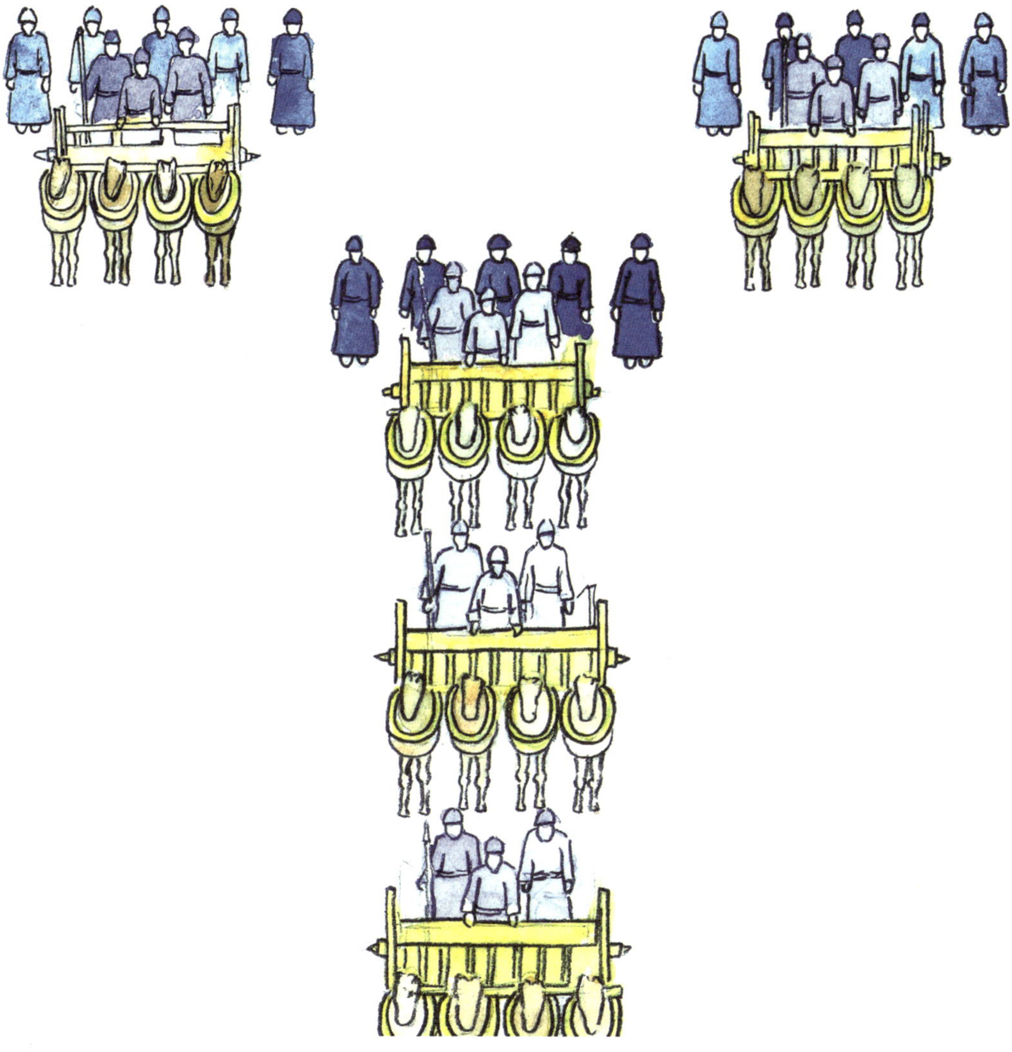

中国古代车战的基本队形（图片提供：FOTOE）
Basic Array of Chariot Battle in Ancient China

定的方法，按照一定的目标来进行训练，以提高士兵的军事素质和加强士兵的团结。在提高军事素质上，李靖提出可分三个阶段训练士兵，如同今天由单兵到多兵、由小分队到大部队、由分练到合练(包括演习)的循序渐进的训练方法。此外，《李卫公问对》也十分重视阵法训练，从理论和实战角度对各种阵法进行了详细的解说。

education and training. It raises the theory that the military education should follow particular approach according to the specific goals to promote soldiers' skill and unity. As to the development of military quality, Li Jing pointed out the three-phase training: from single to group, from small tea to bigger troop, from single practice to joint practice (including military drill), which can train the soldiers step by step. Besides, it also emphasizes the array practice, especially gives several detailed explanation on various array from theoretical and practical perspectives.

> 《太白阴经》

《太白阴经》，全称《神机制敌太白阴经》，是晚唐时期的一部综合性兵书，全书共十卷，两万多字，内容丰富，包括心术、谋略、治军、选将、用兵、武器、通信、行军、宿营、阵法、军用文书、战马、军仪典礼等。该兵书最大的创新之处体现在体例上。该书将军事分解为诸多专题，进行分门别类的研究，为后世兵书的著述开辟了一个新的途径和视野。此外，《太白阴经》具有浓厚的朴素唯物史观和军事辩证法思想，亦堪称是一部哲学著作。

作者简介

《太白阴经》的作者是唐代晚期著名的道教思想理论家、兵学家

> Taibai Yin's Classic

Taibai Yin's Classic, with the full name as *Miraculous Winning Taibai Yin's Classic*, was a comprehensive military book in the late Tang Dynasty (618-907), with total 10 volumes and more than 20,000 characters. It includes various aspects, including mental analysis, strategy, military management, officer selection, military operation, weapon, communication, marching and camping, array, military document, war horse, military manner, etc. The most original character of this book reflects on its compiling style: it divides the military activity into several subjects and gives detailed explanation respectively, which creates a new approach and vision for later generations. Additionally, *Taibai Yin's Classic* bears simple historical materialism and military dialectics thoughts, so it also can be considered as a

李筌（生卒年不详）。据记载，李筌精通文墨，曾担任军政要职。后入名山访道，不知所往。李筌一生著有多部书籍，除《太白阴经》外，还有《阴符经注疏》、《骊山

《太白阴经》之意

在中国古代，太白星是天上众多星宿中的一个，也就是今人所称的金星。古时候，金星有两个名字，人们把早晨所见的东方的金星称为启明星，黄昏所见的西方的金星称为太白星。中国古代以星象来占卜吉凶，而太白星则主杀伐、战事。《太白阴经》中的“太白”正是此意。“阴”则指兵家的阴谋诡道之术，有智慧、谋略之意。

Meaning of *Taibai Yin's Classic*

In ancient China, Venus (called TaiBai in ancient China) is one out of many constellations. In ancient times, Venus had two names: Qiming Star in the dawn and Taibai Star in the dusk. Ancient Chinese people usually conducted divination based on the star images. And Taibai Star represents killing and battles. So the *Taibai* in the book name indicates military activities. And *Yin* indicates the conspiracy and scheme plotted by strategists, meaning wisdom and tactics.

philosophy canon.

Biography

Taibai Yin's Classic, was written by a famous theorist of Taoism and strategist Li Quan (unknown dates of birth and death) in the late Tang Dynasty. According to the record, Li Quan excelled in writing and once served in important position in the army. When he got old, he lived in seclusion in famous mountain. Li Quan wrote many books in his life. Besides *Taibai Yin's Classic*, there includes *Scriptures' Comments of Yin Tally*, *Secrets of Yin Tally Inherited from Mother in Lishan Mountain*, *Qing Nang Kuo*, *Book of Zhong Tai*, *Kun Wai Chun Qiu*, *Liu Ren Da Yu Zhang Ge*, *Annotations for Master Sun's Art of War*, etc.

Major Military Theory

Li Quan emphasizes to exert people's subjective initiative and raised the winning theory that tactic is the most important, meaning the natural elements like weather, climate, and terrain are not the crucial factors to affect the result of the war and destiny of the country. Only relying on people's tactics and releasing potential abilities, the one can seize the victory. Li Quan also thought that there

母传阴符玄义》、《青囊括》、《中台志》、《阃外春秋》、《六壬大玉帐歌》、《孙子注》等。

主要军事思想

李筌非常注重发挥人的主观能动性，提出“人谋上”的制胜论。

is nobody born in valiance or timidity. Whether he or she is brave largely depends on the nurture and training instead of the growing environment. Soldicrs' valiance lies in the tactics applied by the officer. And the combat capacity rests with the situation built by the leader. If the strategy is appropriate,

- 《双骑图》（唐代 韦偃）

画中展现了两个骑士各乘一马，在辽阔的原野上驰骋的情景。

Two Horses, by Wei Yan (Tang Dynasty, 618-907)

It depicts two cavaliers riding their own horse, dashing on the vast grassland.

即天时地利等自然因素都不是决定战争的胜败、国家的存亡的关键，只有依靠人的谋略，充分发挥人的潜能，才能取得战争的胜利。李筌还认为，人没有天生的勇敢和怯懦，是否勇敢也与生长的地方无关，而在于后天的培养和锻炼。士卒的勇敢和怯懦在于将领谋略的运用是否成功，战斗力的强大与薄弱在于将领营造的态势是否有利。只

even the timid soldier can act bravely.

Taibai Yin's Classic, states that the soldier is the main body of the war, who exerts significant influence on the result. Therefore, the selection of the soldier is very important. Only the versatile candidate can be brought into, who should possess the following characteristics: the

• **薛仁贵**

薛仁贵（614-683），唐代名将，武艺高强，统帅指挥能力超强，一生军功赫赫。

Portrait of Xue Rengui

Xue Rengui (614-683), a famous general in the Tang Dynasty, excelled in military operation and achieved numerous military exploits.

• **尉迟恭**

尉迟恭（585—658），唐代名将，勇武善战，屡立战功，曾帮助唐太宗李世民夺取帝位。

Portrait of Yuchi Gong

Yuchi Gong (585-658), a famous general in the Tang Dynasty, who was valiant and resourceful and achieved numerous military exploits. He once assisted Emperor Taizong, Li Shimin ascend to the throne.

- **古练兵场遗址**（图片提供：微图）
Site of Ancient Drill Ground

要谋略得当，那么怯懦的士兵也会变得很勇敢。

《太白阴经》认为，士兵是战争中的主体，对战争的成败具有重要的作用，因此要十分重视对士兵的选拔，要选择多才多艺的士兵。多才多艺的士兵主要指以下这几种类型："智能之士"，即极具智慧、深谋远虑的士兵；"辩说之士"，即极具外交能力的士兵；

resourceful who is extremely intelligent and forethoughtful, the eloquent who possesses the diplomatic ability, the spy who can alienate the enemy and pry for the intelligence, the guide who is very familiar with the battle field, the skillful who possess the ability to produce sharp weapons, the valiant who has a strong body, the motivated who excels in horse riding and climbing city walls, the runner who can walk fast and provide useful

"间谍之士"，即能够离间敌国君臣和窥探敌国情报的士兵；"乡导之士"，即非常熟悉地形和道路状况的士兵；"技巧之士"，即具有高超技术，可以制造锋利的兵器的士兵；"猛毅之士"，即体魄强健的士兵；"矫捷之士"，即善于骑马、能翻越城墙的身手敏捷的士兵；"疾足之士"，即走路速度很快，可以迅速为军队提供情报的士兵；"巨力之士"，即能够承担重物的士兵；"技术之士"，即懂得阴阳五行之说的士兵。

《太白阴经》指出，注重刑赏是统兵作战的将领必须学会的重要技能。不能徇私情而奖赏无功之人，不能因私怨而对无罪之人进行处罚。将领掌握着士兵们的生杀大权，不可差之毫厘，要尽最大的可能做到"赏一功而千万人悦，刑一罪而千万人慎"。

information, the powerful who can bear heavy things, the diviner who knows how to conduct divination.

Taibai Yin's Classic points out that a good leader should learn to reward and punish the soldiers appropriately and fairly. He cannot practice favoritism and grant reward to the man who achieved nothing, cannot punish the innocent out of personal grudge. The leader holds the scale of the rules and should not act inappropriately. The officer should try to attain the result that rewarding one person then the other feel happy for him and punishing one person when the other act cautiously.

>《武经总要》

《武经总要》是中国第一部由官方修编的兵书，也是中国最早的军事百科全书。全书共四十卷，约二十五万字，并配有三百多张图片加以说明。内容主要包括选将练兵、部队编制、通信侦察、军事地形、古今阵法、战略战术、城池攻防、边疆政策等。《武经总要》在中国兵书编纂史上具有重要的影响，它丰富和发展了兵书的体例和学科门类的设置，同时开创了在军事理论研究中对地理志进行研究的先河。

作者简介

《武经总要》由官方修订，主持者为曾公亮和丁度两位北宋官员。曾公亮（999 1078），著名的

> *Main Points in Military Theory*

Main Points in Military Theory, is the first military book issued by government in China, also is the first military encyclopedia, with 40 volumes and about 250,000 characters as well as more than 300 illustrations. It includes several aspects including officer selection and military training, military organization, communication, military terrain, military array, strategy and tactics, city attack and defense, frontier policy, etc. *Main Points in Military Theory* has exerted great influence on the history of the military books' compilation in China, which enriched and developed the style of military books and the subject set, as well as initiated the study on geography in military theories.

• 北宋初期的战争场景
Battle Field in the Early Northern Song Dynasty (960-1127)

政治家、军事家、军火家，在朝廷任职期间致力于革弊兴利，深受百姓爱戴。丁度（990—1053），著名的文字训诂学家。曾公亮和丁度受任编纂《武经总要》后，精选八方人才，广采博录，共用五年时间完成此书。

主要军事思想

自春秋战国以来，军事家们都在不断的论证战争的必要性，《武经总要》继承并修正了这一观点，

Biography

Main Points in Military Theory was compiled by the government, which was commissioned by two officials Zeng Gongliang and Ding Du in the Northern Song Dynasty (960-1127). Zeng Gongliang (999-1078), a famous politician, strategist and munitions expert, in his service in the courtyard, he was dedicated to the political reform, which earned him the public support. Ding Du (990-1053), a famous expert in the explanation of Chinese characters in

采石之战

公元1161年，金国60万大军攻打南宋，试图从采石矶（长江东岸，今安徽省马鞍山市西南）渡江南侵，虞允文率军阻截。战前，虞允文一方面安抚民众，一方面召集前线将领，说以忠义，动员宋兵团结一致共御强敌。宋兵士气大振，决心与金军决一死战。

虞允文命令步兵、骑兵沿江布阵，又将水军分为五队，一队在江中，两队在两翼岸边，另外两队在山后设伏。当地的民兵和群众自发运输粮草，协助宋军作战。金军渡江时，没有料到宋军会奋力抵抗，一时之间被水陆两军打得措手不及。而宋军充分利用水军的优势，成功地在江面截断金军船只。金军不善水战，船舰落后，一时处于劣势。待到天黑，虞允文命一队宋军挥舞战旗、猛擂战鼓，佯装有援兵到达，金军吓得闻风而逃。虞允文乘胜追击，水路配合，再度大败金军。

在这场战役中，宋军深得民心，得到了民众的帮助，而将领虞允文也机智果敢，指挥得当，最终才得以取胜。

Battle of Caishi

In 1161, the Jin Dynasty (1115-1234) launched a war to the Southern Song Dynasty with 600,000 soldiers and tried to invade the Southern Song via Caishiji (today's southwestern area in Ma'anshan City in Anhui Province, on the east bank of the Yangtze River). Yu Yunwen led army to resist the attack. Before the battle, Yu Yunwen tried to comfort the people and also summoned the soldiers at the front to encourage them with loyalty and righteousness to make them keep united. Then the soldiers in the Song's army were fully prepared and swore to fight against the enemy till the death.

Yu Yunwen arranged the infantries and cavalries along the river and divided the water army into five teams: one was in the river; two were at flanks; another two ambushed behind the mountains. The local soldiers and people

• 南宋车船（模型）

Wheeled Ship (Southern Song Dynasty, 1127-1279)(Model)

volunteered to assist the delivery of army provisions. While Jin's army crossing the river, they never expected a furious resistance. In the panic, they couldn't cope with Song's sudden attack. While Song's water army took the advantages and successfully captured Jin's boats. Jin's soldiers were not good at water battle. Due to the lost of boats, they were in the disadvantage. In the night, Yu Yunwen ordered a team to wave the banners and beat the drums to pretend the arrival of the reinforcement, which scared Jin's army away instantly. Yu Yunwen pursued the remnant troops and defeated the Jin's army once again.

In this battle, Song's army had the public support and was a justice army. The leader Yu Yunwen was also resourceful and courageous. So they won the war.

认为战争是必要的，但是进行战争时必须“以仁义为本，以权谋为用”。只有以仁义为本的国家，才能做到安抚民众、悦服豪杰，才具有战胜敌人的坚实基础。统兵作战的将帅只有以仁义为本，才能使三军亲附，使士卒勇于奋战。

在以往的军事理论中，军事家很少提到有关兵器制造的问题的，而《武经总要》则明确提出了“器利而工善”的兵器制造理论。该理论认为，强大的军队只有使用精致而适用的兵器，才能战胜劲敌。如果士兵披着的铠甲不坚实，那就好像赤膊袒胸一样不能保护身体；如果士兵手握的武器不够精良，那就好像赤手空拳一样不能给敌人以致命的打击。因此，兵器是军队发挥

ancient books. Zeng Gongliang and Ding Du were appointed to compile the book *Main Points in Military Theory*. They selected the talent across the country and spent five years to complete this book.

Major Military Theory

Since the Spring and Autumn Period (770 B.C.-476 B.C.) and Warring States Period (475 B.C.-221 B.C.), strategists were constantly discussing the necessity of the war. *Main Points in Military Theory* inherited and revised their points: the war is necessary. However, it must be based on justice and righteousness and carried out with strategies. Only the country based on justice and righteousness can comfort the people and earn the admiration from the heroes, and then has the solid foundation for the victory.

唧筒：原始活塞机械。
Valve: primitive valve mechanical device.

油柜：用来储放燃料。
Oil Tank: storing fuel.

火楼：内部盛放有引火药。
Fire Jar: storing the ignition charge.

- **宋代猛火油柜（模型）**

猛火油柜是一种喷火兵器，也是世界上最早的火焰喷射器，在古代城邑攻防作战中可以烧伤敌人，甚至焚毁兵器，具有巨大威力。据《武经总要》记载，猛火油柜以猛火油（石油）为燃料，用熟铜做柜。发射时，点燃火楼中的引火药，火楼体内温度升高，通过热传导预热油缸前的喷油通道，形成预热区。这时用力抽拉唧筒，使油柜中的压强改变，从而将猛火油经过火楼喷出。

Firing Oil Tank in the Song Dynasty(Model)

The firing oil tank was a type of fire arm, also was the earliest flamethrower in the world. In the city attack or defense battle in ancient times, it was extremely powerful and can be applied to injure the enemy, even destroy their weapons. According to the *Main Points in Military Theory*, the firing oil tank was fueled with fossil oil. In the attack, the one should light the ignition charge inside the fire jar. Then the inner temperature raises and preheats the oil injection channel through heat conduction to form a preheating zone. Then, drag the piston valve to change the air pressure inside the tank and spray the heated oil from the spout.

火药与火器

火药是中国古代四大发明之一。它是由硝石、硫黄、木炭混合而成，点燃后能迅速燃烧或引发爆炸。因硝石、硫黄在中国古代都是药典中记录的药物，故称为“火药”。

秦汉时期，帝王贵胄为求不死，命方士炼制长生金丹。方士在尝试了大量原料后，从各类失败的燃烧爆炸丹方中总结经验，发明了火药。10至14 世纪战争频繁，用于军事的火器随之出现。南宋后期，由于火药性能的提高，出现了以火药为能源的弹丸发射器。元代，在以往火药技术的基础上，出现了具有现代枪械雏形的新式兵器——火铳。元末明初，明太祖朱元璋将火铳广泛用于陆战攻坚与水战之中。明成祖朱棣还组建了全部用火器武装起来的特殊部队“神机营”。

明代中期，传承旧制的火药兵器没有大的突破，直到欧洲先进的枪和炮制造技术传到中国后，明代的远射兵器才获得了很大发展。清代中期后，中国的火器技术故步自封，即不提倡改革，又排斥外来技术，火器发展渐趋停止。

- **红夷炮**

“红夷炮”是明代对从欧洲传入的大型前装火炮的通称。17世纪初，荷兰殖民者曾多次侵犯中国沿海地区，并用一种大炮攻击明军，中国人称其为“红夷炮”。从此，中国开始仿制这种火炮。

Red Foreign Cannon

“Red Foreign Cannon” was the general term for the large front loading cannon which was introduced from Europe in the Ming Dynasty. In the early 17 century, the colonist from Netherlands repetitively invaded the coastal region of China and used the cannon to attack Ming's army. People called the cannon the Red Foreign Cannon. Since then, Chinese started to duplicate such kind of cannon.

Gunpowder and Firearm

Gunpowder is one of the Four Great Inventions in ancient China, which is made up by saltpeter, sulfur and charcoal. After being ignited, it burns rapidly and triggers the explosion. As saltpeter and sulfur are medicines recorded in Chinese medical canons, hence the name fire medicine.

In the Qin Dynasty (221 B.C.-206 B.C.) and Han Dynasty (206 B.C.-220 A.D.), the emperors wanted to achieve the immortality. So they ordered the alchemists to make the golden elixirs. The alchemist tried numerous materials and concluded several experiences out of the failed cases and invented the gunpowder. Due to the continuous wars in the 10th-14th century, the firearm also appeared. In the late Southern Song Dynasty, due to the promotion of the gunpowder's performance, there appeared the projectile launching device driven by gunpowder. In the Yuan Dynasty (1279-1368), on the basis of the former techniques, it appeared a new weapon called fire case (*Huo Chong*) which resembled the primitive gun device. In the late Yuan Dynasty, Emperor Taizu of the Ming Dynasty (1368-1644), Zhu Yuanzhang repetitively applied the fire case in the fortress attack and water attack. Emperor Chengzu of the Ming Dynasty, Zhu Di also organized a special force armed with fire arms called "mysterious battalion".

In the middle period of the Ming Dynasty, the firearm produced according to the ancient designs didn't have any breakthrough. Until the advanced production techniques of guns and cannons were introduced from Europe to China, the long shot weapon didn't have any further development in the Ming Dynasty. In the late Qing Dynasty, the evolution of production technique of firearms ceased and the government rejected the foreign techniques, which led the cease of the development of firearms.

明神机营装备的铁炮

Iron Cannon Equipped in Mysterious Battalion (Ming Dynasty, 1368-1644)

勇猛战斗力的重要条件，制造者必须精益求精，不可有丝毫马虎。

《武经总要》还记录了火药的配方和火器的制造方法，这是世界上最早的火药制造配方。

《武经总要》中记述的蒺藜火球（模型）

蒺藜火球是宋代出现的带有棘刺杀伤物的球状抛掷火器，点燃后用炮掷入敌船或敌营以纵火。

Caltrop Fire Ball Depicted in the *Main Points in Military Theory* (Model)

Caltrop fire ball was a globular cast firearm with thorns invented in the Song Dynasty. After being lit, it will be projected with cannon towards the enemy's warships or camps.

The leader should act according to the principle of justice and righteousness, then he can earn the support and make the soldier fight for him bravely.

In the former military theories, the strategist rarely mentioned the issues about weapon production. However, *Main Points in Military Theory* explicitly raises the weapon production theory that well-functioned weapon can raise the efficiency. It indicates that the powerful army should use exquisite and appropriate weapons to achieve the victory. If the armor is not firm enough then it can not protect the soldier. If the weapon is not good enough then it is like the soldier fight with their bare hands and can not gives the enemy the vital hit. Therefore, weapon is an important part to develop soldiers' fighting capacity. The producer must be meticulous and pursue the perfection.

Main Points in Military Theory also records the production method of gunpowder and firearm, which was the earliest formula for the gunpowder.

陈家岛海战

《武经总要》中重视兵器制造的思想，在陈家岛海战之中得到了很好的运用。南宋绍兴三十一年（1161），金国军队大举攻宋，大将李宝由海路北上，迎击南侵的金军水师。李宝抓住战机，在陈家岛水域（属黄海海域）命水师包围金军，用新创制的火药箭与火球，从四面环射金军战船，歼灭了金军。陈家岛海战是世界战争史上最早将火药箭、火球与冷兵器结合使用的一次水战。

Naval Battle of Chens' Isles

In the *Main Points in Military Theory*, it emphasizes the production of weapons which can be reflected in the Naval Battle of Chens' Isles. In 1161, the Jin Dynasty launched a war to the Southern Song Dynasty, the general Li Bao went north via the sea to resist the navy of the Jin Dynasty. Li Bao took the opportunity and besieged Jin's navy at Chens' Isles (in Yellow Sea) and used the newly developed fire arrow and fire ball to attack the enemy's warships and defeat Jin's navy completely. It was the first time the fire arrow and fire ball applied with the cold weapons in a naval battle in the world military history.

- **《武经总要》中记述的毒药烟球（模型）**

毒药烟球是一种可散放毒烟的球状抛掷火器。点燃后毒药烟球逐层燃烧，能产生大量有毒浓烟，可迷晕或毒死敌人。

Poisonous Smoking Ball Depicted in the *Main Points in Military Theory* (Model)

Poisonous smoking ball was a globular smoking toxic cast firearm. After being lit, the ball will start burning layer by layer and produce numerous toxic smoke to stun or kill the enemy.

> 《守城录》

《守城录》是南宋时期刊行的一部论述城邑防御的专著，也是中国古代影响最大、价值最高的城防专著。该书将理论和实践相结合，系统阐述了城防理论和守城战的各个方面。全书由三部分组成，共四卷，约1.8万字。《守城录》的内容主要包括改革旧城制、增开城门、改造和创制新型守城兵器等，多被明清时期研究城防者所引用。

作者简介

《守城录》的作者是陈规和汤琫。陈规（1072—1141），宋代著名的抗金将领、军事家。陈规文韬武略兼备，精通军事兵法，喜藏书，是最早研制和使用管形火器的人。他发明的用大竹筒装填火药以

> Book of City Defense

Book of City Defense, is a military canon exclusively for city defense issued in the Southern Song Dynasty (1127-1279), also is the one with the greatest influence and highest value in this domain. This book combines the theory with the actual practice and systematically states the theories of city defense in several aspects. This book has three parts, with total four volumes and 18,000 characters, including reforming the old city planning, adding new gates, reforming and innovating new defense weapons, which are broadly referred by the scholars studying in city defense in the Ming Dynasty (1368-1644) and Qing Dynasty (1644-1911).

Biography

Book of City Defense was written by Chen Gui and Tang Shu. Chen Gui (1072-1141), a famous military officer in

• **东京保卫战**

宋宣和七年（1125），金兵南下侵宋，包围了北宋都城东京（今河南开封）。大臣李纲积极组织军民备战，修楼橹，安炮座，设弩床，运砖石，备火油……准备了许多防守器械，最终击退了金军。

Self-defensive Battle of Dongjing

In 1125, Jin's army invaded the Song Dynasty from the north and besieged the capital city of Northern Song Dynasty (today's Kaifeng City in Henan Province). The patriot official Li Gang actively organized the soldiers and common people to prepare the war. They built the observation towers and turrets, set the crossbow base and carrying the bricks and rocks, prepared the firing oil and many defensive devices. Finally, they defeated the Jin's army.

喷射火焰的火枪，应用于后世的战争之中。汤璹，生卒年不详，宋光宗绍熙四年（1193）他将自己写成的《建炎德安守御录》两卷上呈给朝廷。后来，宋宁宗下令将此书与陈规所作的《〈靖康朝野佥言〉后

the Song Dynasty, who excelled in the tactics and military strategies and was fond of collecting books. He was the first man inventing and using the tubular firearms. The firelock he invented storing the gunpowder in its thick bamboo tube was applied in the battle by the later

序》和《守城机要》合并，汇编为《守城录》。

主要军事思想

北宋后期直至南宋，金国始终对大宋虎视眈眈，经常率军攻打宋朝城池。靖康二年（1127），金国灭掉了北宋，将原都城汴京改为

• **宋代塞门刀车（模型）**

塞门刀车是当所守城门被攻破时，守军用来堵塞城门的守城器械。

Gate Blocking Device: Knife Cart in the Song Dynasty (Model)

The gate blocking device, knife cart was used by the defenders to block the city gate while the enemy attacked.

generations. Tang Shu, unknown dates of birth and death, presented his work Jianyan *De'an Defense Guidebook* (2 volumes) to Emperor Guangzong in 1193. Later Emperor Ningzong ordered to compile this book with *The Epilogue of the Collection of Conversation in Jingkang's Courtyard* and *City Defense Guidebook*, by Chen Gui together into *Book of City Defense*.

Major Military Theory

From the late Northern Song Dynasty to the Southern Song Dynasty, the Jin Dynasty in the north had been coveted Song Dynasty and often attacked Song's cities. In 1127, Jin overturned the Northern Song Dynasty and changed the original capital city Bianjing into Kaifeng Administrative Office in Nanjing as the auxiliary capital to the Jin Dynasty. In the *Book of City Defense*, the author analyzed this situation and pointed out that although the Kaifeng City was huge and firm, yet there were lack of the efficient attack device and operation tactics targeting the Jin's army, therefore, Song's army could not resist Jin's attack. If the defenders could heighten and thicken the walls and strengthen them with huge plank, then it would largely decrease the casualty. *Book*

- **宋代云梯（模型）**

  云梯是一种用以攀越城墙的攻城兵器。

  Scaling Ladder in the Song Dynasty (Model)

  The scaling ladder was a device used for the city attack to help the soldiers climbing the walls

“南京开封府”，作为金国陪都。《守城录》分析了这一现状，指出开封城虽然大且坚固，但没有针对金军的攻城器械和战法，因而无法有效地阻止金军的进攻。如果守城者能够及时将城墙加高、加厚，再用大木加固，就不会有如此重大的伤亡了。《守城录》中列举了多种改善城防建设的举措，指出要根据实战需要进行城墙改建。

- **宋代撞车（模型）**

  撞车是中国古代战争中的攻城工具之一。攻城的时候，可以用撞车撞击城门或城墙，以便在城防中打开缺口，让步兵或骑兵攻入城中。

  Banging Cart in the Song Dynasty (Model)

  The banging cart was used in the city attack in ancient war in China. While attacking the city, soldiers could use the cart knock the gate or the wall to open a crack in the defense line and create a passageway for the infantries and cavalries.

of City Defense also provides various measures to improve the city defense and points out it should rebuild the wall in accordance with the actual needs or situation in the war.

The rock projector was a long-distance cast weapon used in the city

抛石机是用来攻、守城堡的远程抛射武器。早在大炮诞生之前，人们就已使用抛石机向敌人投掷巨石了。《守城录》对抛石机守城制敌的技术和战术提出了创造性的见解：聘请技精艺熟的能工巧匠，选取坚实的材料来制作投石机，同时还要对士兵进行训练，以便在作战时熟练地抛击敌人。

attack and defense. Before the birth of the cannon, people already used the rock projector in the battle. *Book of City Defense* raises an original theory on the production technique and military tactics of rock projector: hire skillful craftsmen to choose firm and hard material to make the projector, meanwhile, train the soldiers to prepare for the actual war against the enemy.

轴：在木结构的架上横置的可转动的轴，将炮梢装在轴上。

Axis: The rotatable axis installed on the wooden frames, on which the cannon can be installed.

架：用坚硬的木料制成，有的架下安装有轮子，可以移动。

Frame: It was made from hard wood installed wheels below to make it movable.

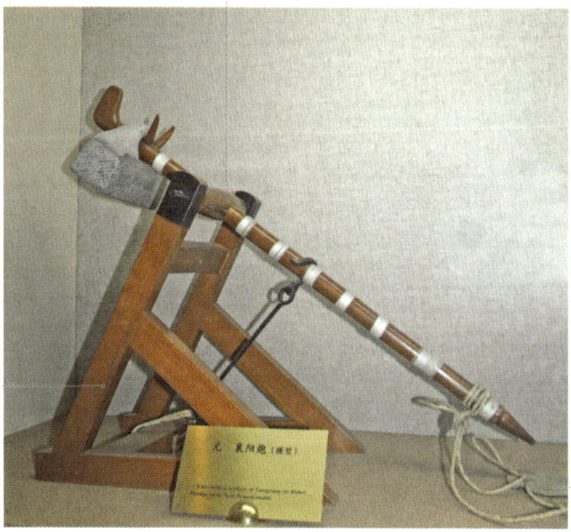

皮窝：用来兜装炮弹。

Leather Nest: It was used to wrap the cannonball.

抛石机（模型）

Rock Projector (Model)

改造德安城

靖康元年(1126)，陈规任德安县令，上任后便开始全力加强城防，改造城池，创制了长杆火枪，改进了抛石机。从靖康元年到绍兴二年(1126—1132)，金军不断地进犯德安，陈规率军“九攻九拒，应敌无穷”。当时，中原州郡几乎全部被金军攻陷，只有德安城仍然固守。

陈规根据金军作战的特点，对德安城进行了如下改造：

1.将原来的女墙改成平头形女墙。德安城原来的女墙比较矮且墙体较薄，陈规认为这样的女墙是无法发挥防御作用的，便将原来的女墙加高加厚，改造成了平头形的女墙。

2.加强城门的防御设施。旧时德安城城门的防御措施不够强大，防御外敌入侵的效果很弱。为此陈规对其进行改造：在城门顶上建立了双层城楼；废弃了原来的瓮城，改成了护门墙；增修了暗墙，这样可以在敌人攻破外层护城墙时起到阻止敌军进入城内的作用。

3.改建城墙四角。城墙的四角历来是人们忽视的地方，而陈规却异常重视城墙四角的作用。陈规将德安城城墙的四角进行了改建，将原来的直角改为弧形角，东北角为内凹圆弧，其余三角为外凸圆弧。这种城角便于两面守军相互照应，也便从后侧杀伤攻城的敌人，扩大了攻击面积。

床弩（模型）

床弩在宋代守城战中应用较为广泛，是一种装在床架上的大型弩，以绞动后部轮轴的方式张弓装箭，待机发射。

Bedstead Crossbow (Model)

The bedstead crossbow was broadly used in the city defense in the Song Dynasty (960-1279). It was a large crossbow installed on the bedstead and bend the crossbow by winding the axles at the end and wait the signal for launching.

Reform of De'an City

In 1126, Chen Gui was appointed as the county magistrate in De'an. When he assumed the office, he started to enhance the city defense and reform the city walls. He created the long-arm firelock and improved the rock projector. From 1126 to 1132, the Jin's army constantly harassed the De'an City. Chen Gui led the army protect the city for nine times. At that time, almost all the states and counties in the Central Plains were taken by Jin's army. Only the De'an City survived.

Chen Gui conducted following reforms according to the operation style of Jin's army:

1.Change the original parapet wall into flat-end wall. The original walls of the De'an City were short and thin. Chen Gui thought it could not protect the city efficiently, so he heightened and thickened the old walls and replaced them into flat-end walls.

2.Enhance the defensive devices. The defensive measures of the old De'an City were vulnerable and inefficient. So Chen Gui built a two-storey gate tower on the gate and abandoned the original barbican entrance and rebuilt them into guarding gates, also built additional walls which could protect the city while the outer walls were broken.

3.Rebuild the four corners of the city. The four corners of the city have been easily ignored by people. However, Chen Gui paid much attention on the function of the corners. He rebuilt the four corners from the original right angle into arc-shaped corners. The northeast corner was indent arc; other three corners were protruding arcs. This structure made the defenders on the flanks communicate with each other more easily and also can allow the defenders attack the enemy soldiers from the rear side and expanse the attack area.

• 用于攻城的踏橛箭
Stepping Arrows Used in City Attack

> 《南船记》

《南船记》是一本战船建造专著，其主要内容是关于战船的建造、用途和管理方式等的论述。书中记载了各种类型的战船，包括黄船、战巡船、桥船、后湖船、快船等，并记载了各类战船的船形、各个组成部分的构件、各种船具的尺寸，以及建造时所需的材料数量等内容，对当时及后世的造船业产生了很大的影响。

作者简介

《南船记》的作者是明代杰出的水利与战船建造专家沈𡸁。沈𡸁生于弘治四年（1491），曾在朝为官，政绩甚佳，能解百姓疾苦，终因得罪缙绅而被罢官。沈𡸁晚年时隐居深山，潜心著书。

> Book of Shipbuilding in Nanjing

Book of Shipbuilding in Nanjing, is a military book exclusively about warship building, with the content mainly about the construction, application and the management of the warships. It records various warships, including yellow warship, cruiser warship, bridge warship, lake warship and fast warship and also depicts their structures and components, as well as the size of the ship's instruments and the quantity of the material required at that time, which exerts great influence on the shipbuilding industry in later generations.

Biography

Book of Shipbuilding in Nanjing was written by Shen Qi, an outstanding warship constructer in the Ming Dynasty (1368-1644). He was born in 1491

主要军事思想

《南船记》指出，凡是濒江临海地区和水网地带，就难以避免有水上战事发生。明朝虽已统一全国，但东南沿海和江淮之地一旦发生战乱，便会牵动全国。所以沿海地带必须居安思危、建造战船，供官兵平时进行作战训练之用。建造

and once served in the courtyard with good reputation. He helped the people and acted uprightly, then finally was dismissed from the office as he annoyed the local retired officials. Shen Qi lived in the remote mountain in his late years and concentrated on reading and writing.

Major Military Theory

Book of Shipbuilding in Nanjing points out that the areas near the river or the sea coast or other water systems, are suffered from the harassments from the water. Although the Ming Dynasty is a united country, if there are conflicts breaking out in the south-east coastal areas and the areas along the Yangtze River and Huai River, it might evolve into severe situation. So the coastal areas should prepare the chaos in advance and build the warships for training in peacetime. The shipbuilding should learn from the former regulations, rules and experiences, also needs some changes

- **艨艟（模型）**

艨艟是一种以速度快而著称的轻型战船，结构轻巧，机动灵活，便于机动作战。艨艟以生牛皮蒙背，利于冲波破浪，具有良好的防御性能。其前后左右都有弩窗，可以四面发射弓弩。

Warship Covered with Cowhide (Model)

It was a light warship which was famous for its speed, with simple structure and flexible motivation. It was mainly used in the motive battle. The ship was covered with cowhide which was convenient for him to ride on the waves and provides good defensive performance. There were crossbow windows around the ship to allow it attack from four sides.

- **斗舰**

斗舰是一种装备较好的轻型战船，船上设有女墙，高约三尺，女墙上设有箭孔，可以放箭攻击敌人。船尾处设有高台，士兵可以在这里观察水面情形。

Fight Warship

The fight warship is a well-equipped light warship, with parapet wall (about one meter high) on which there are arrow holes for attack. There sets a tower at the end of the ship on which the soldier can observe the situation on the water.

- **明代海军的指挥船（模型）**

Command Vessel in the Ming Dynasty (Model)

战船既要吸取历代的规制、法则和有益的经验，又要因时而变，遵循“尽变通之利”这一原则。造船与制造其他器物一样，若要充分发挥它的作用，就必须要按时代的需要进行改造。

《南船记》认为，水战和陆战一样，都要采用灵活的阵法。战船的船体长短宽窄各有不同，只有将各种类型的战船混合编队，灵活布阵，才能获得水战的胜利。

depending on the actual situations. Abide by the principle of keeping flexible. The shipbuilding is similar to other production industries. In order to exert its function, it needs continuous reforms to meet the needs of different periods.

Book of Shipbuilding in Nanjing, states that the water battle is the same with the field battle, which all require flexible tactics. The warships have different sizes and are varied in type, which allow the leader create flexible tactics and formations to win the battle.

《龙江船厂志》

《龙江船厂志》也是一部专门论述战船建造和船厂管理的专著，为明代专理船政的官员李昭祥所著。李昭祥认为，建造军用船只要坚持战船与巡船并举的方针，以防止敌军突然来袭。水军在操练时，进退快慢都要按军律进行。《龙江船厂志》中还概述了明代以前水战之事以及所建造的战船，其中提到的著名战船和战具有上百种，并创造出适应新时期需要的多种新式战船。

Journal of Longjiang Shipyard

Journal of Longjiang Shipyard, is another shipbuilding book depicting the construction methods and the management of the shipyard. It was written by Li Zhaoxiang, an official exclusively in charge of the shipbuilding. Li believed that warship building should stick to the principle of keeping the balance of the warship and cruiser in case the enemy's raid. While practicing, the movement and the speed should be controlled and performed according to the orders. This book also concludes all the water battles before the Ming Dynasty as well as the warships built before, including hundreds of famous warships and weapons. Based on the former structure and experience, the author created various new-style warships according to the actual situations.

> 《纪效新书》

《纪效新书》是一部关于练兵、治军及兵器研制的专著。该兵书虽是为荡平倭寇（日本海盗）而撰写的，但内容非常丰富，全面介绍了练兵和治军的意义、原则和方法。此外，《纪效新书》以通俗易懂的口语书写，如同讲课的教本，士兵听后易记易学，又如同是作战训练的条令，方便士兵操作和执行，具有较强的普及性和实用性。

作者简介

《纪效新书》是明代杰出的军事家、抗倭名将戚继光（1528—1587）在平定东南倭患时所著的。嘉靖四十年（1561），戚继光率军在台州地区（今浙江省沿海中部）抗倭，九战九捷。在他的不断努力

> New Theories on Military Training, Strategies and Experience

New Theories on Military Training, Strategies and Experience, is a book exclusively about the military training and weapon production. Although it was mainly for the battles against the Japanese pirates, this book has rich content and fully reflects the meaning, principle and methods of training and tactic teaching. Besides, it was written in the vernacular language like a textbook, which was convenient for the soldiers to study and remember. And it was also like the orders in the training, which made it easier for the soldiers to operate. So it was a universal and practical military handbook.

Biography

New Theories on Military Training,

• 戚继光像（左）
Portrait of Qi Jiguang(left)

下，至嘉靖四十五年（1566），东南沿海的倭患基本平定，明朝的海疆得以廓清。

戚继光不仅是一个伟大的军事实践家，还是一个伟大的军事理论家，创作了《纪效新书》、《练兵实纪》等著名兵书。

主要军事思想

明代倭寇不断侵犯沿海地区，成为朝廷的心腹大患。为了彻底杜

Strategies and Experience, is written by Qi Jiguang (1528-1587), an outstanding strategists and general who fought against the Japanese pirates. It was completed while he was in the war with Japanese on the southeastern areas. In 1561, Qi Jiguang attacked Japanese in Taizhou area (today's middle area along the coast in the Zhejiang Province) and won nine times consecutively. In his effort, by 1566, the trouble caused by the Japanese pirates had been suppressed and the coastal territory had been declared explicitly.

Qi Jiguang was not only a great strategist, but also an excellent military theorist, who wrote many famous military books including *New Theories on Military Training*, *Strategies and Experience* and *Notes on the Military Training*.

Major Military Theory

In the Ming Dynasty, the Japanese pirates constantly harassed the coastal areas, which became a hidden danger and a major issue for the authority. In order to eradicate the harassments, Qi Jiguang raised the theory of coast defense in the book *New Theories on Military Training*,

上峰岭之战

嘉靖四十年（1561），倭寇2000余人欲经上峰岭侵袭台州。戚继光率1500余人，在上峰岭上设伏以待。戚继光探知倭寇的行军特点是首尾皆为精兵强将，中间兵力较弱。于是，他待倭寇前锋经过后才下令攻击，从高处以鸟铳进攻。倭寇四面受敌，猝不及防，败退而逃。这场战争是在山地战中以谋为本、以鸟铳为主要兵器歼灭倭寇的一个出色战例。

Battle of Shangfengling

In 1561, 2,000 Japanese pirates intended to attack the Taizhou City via Shangfengling. Qi Jiguang led 1,500 soldiers and reached Shangfengling preparing to ambush the enemy. Qi Jiguang knew that Japanese pirates would like to set its main force at two ends. The middle part is vulnerable. So he didn't order the attack until the head soldiers passed the valley. Suddenly, thousands of firing arrows shot from the mountains. The Japanese pirates didn't expect the attack and escaped with panic. This ambush was plotted according to the terrain and assisted with the firing arrows, which becomes a famous example.

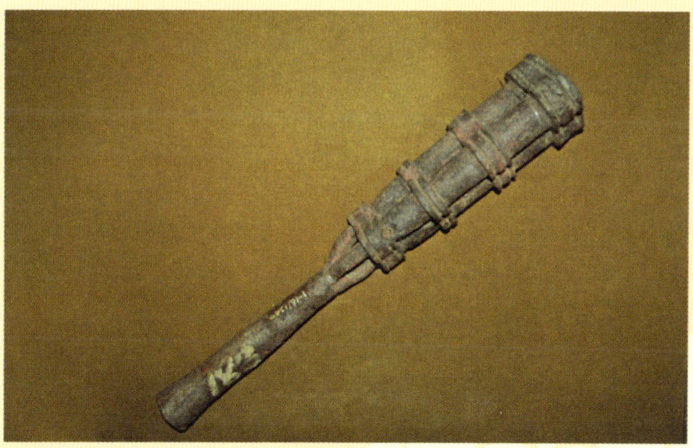

- **明代三眼铳**

三眼铳是一种短火器，以铁或钢铸成，三个铳管可轮番射击。

Three-eyed Fire Case (Ming Dynasty, 1368-1644)

The three-eyed fire case is a short firearm, made from iron or steel, with three tubes for attack.

绝倭寇的侵袭，戚继光在《纪效新书》中提出了“御海洋”的战略思想。他指出，要抵御倭寇，首先就要做好海洋的防御工作。他提出了一系列措施，如大力进行战船建设，一有敌情便出海作战；平日里要加强海上巡逻，并且沿海诸岛要设烽火台，以便于及时通报敌情；修复沿海诸岛早已经名存实亡的水

Strategies and Experience. He believed that the government should prepare for Japanese attacks in advance and enhance the coast defense in the first place. He provided series of measures, including developing the shipbuilding, organizing a naval army to deal with the Japanese pirates, conduct training and cruise in peacetime, setting beacon towers on the isles to report enemy's situation, restoring

- **宁台温大捷**

明嘉靖年间（1522—1566），戚继光在宁台温沿海地区（今属浙江）水路并进，驾福船作战，大败倭寇。

Victory of Ningtaiwen

In 1522-1566, Qi Jiguang led infantries and navies to confront with the Japanese pirates at the coastal area of Ningtaiwien (today's Zhejiang Province) and finally defeated them completely.

明代福船（模型）

福船是明代南海水军的主要战船，福船船高如楼，底尖上阔，首尾高昂，两侧有护板。全船分为四层，下层装土石压舱，二层住兵士，三层是主要操作场所，上层是作战场所。

Blessing Warship in the Ming Dynasty(Model)

The blessing warship is the major warship equipped in the navy in the South China Sea in the Ming Dynasty. It was as large as a tower building, with ogival base and broad top, as well as rising head and end. There were guard boards on the flanks. The ship had four storeys: the lowest storey was used to store soil and rock to keep the ship stable; the second storey had soldiers' cabins; the third storey was the operation room and the upper storey was the battle field.

寨，并备足哨船，这样才能够达到御敌于海洋的目的。

《纪效新书》中提出了许多选兵的标准，指出所选士兵首先要有爱国保家的决心及敢于同敌人拼死战斗的胆量和勇气，此外还要体魄雄伟、武艺高强、头脑灵活。戚继光还强调从严治军，明确各级将领和士兵的职责，上下号令要一致，对士兵的训练要从实战出发，坚决反对搞虚套和花架子。《纪效新

the old water villages on the isles, and preparing enough scout boats. In this way, the coast defense could be enhanced and the areas would be free from the harassments from the Japanese.

New Theories on Military Training, Strategies and Experience, mentions many criterions for soldier selections. It points out that the soldier should be loyal to the country and dare to fight with the enemy till death. Additionally, they should have strong figure, be highly skilled in martial arts and be resourceful. Qi Jiguang also emphasizes the importance of setting strict rules and clarifying the respective responsibilities and abiding by the orders with consistency. The training should follow the actual situations and abandon

狼筅
Wolf Stick

• 戚继光的狼筅兵
Soldiers Holding Wolf Sticks

书》中明确规定：军队训练时，将领和士兵都要戴盔穿甲、执兵器、荷重物；训练的兵器要稍重于交战时使用的兵器；士兵训练时腿上要

the unpractical tricks. *New Theories on Military Training, Strategies and Experience* explicitly stipulates that: in the training, the officers and soldiers should wear armors and holding weapons

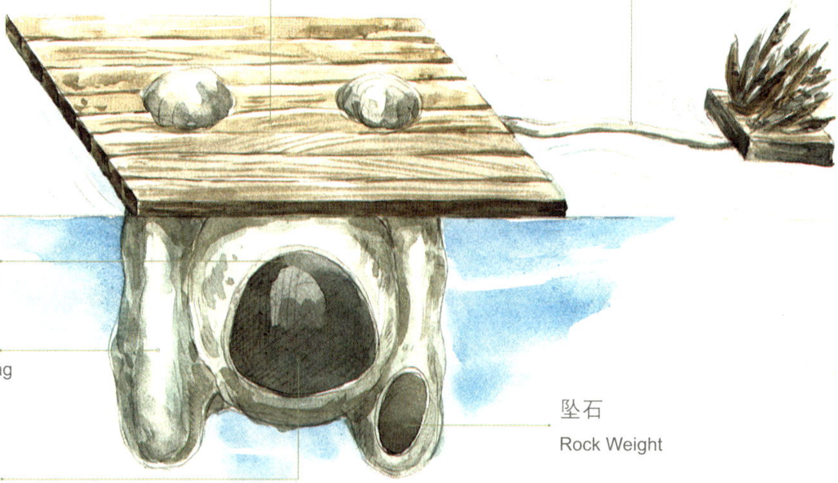

- **龙王炮**

龙王炮是一种定时爆炸水雷，爆炸物是一个铁球，内盛火药，炮口安设香头充做引信，香头的长短根据漂流时间而定。外裹牛皮制的袋子，外表涂油，以防水浸。为了保持袋里有足量的空气以免火种熄灭，用羊肠线接通到用雁翎伪装的另一个木筏上，然后将龙王炮绑在木排下面，系上石坠，使其浮于水中。

Dragon King Bomb

The Dragon King bomb is a timing underwater mine, made up by an iron ball storing gunpowder inside and installed incense tip at the mouth of the bomb serving as the fuse. The size of the incense tip was determined by the drifting time. It is wrapped with cowhide bag and applied with oil to resist the water. In order to keep enough air in the bag to keep the incense tip being quenched, a catgut thread ties it to another raft disguised with goose feather. Then tie the bombs below the raft and add rock weight to keep it afloat in the water.

裹沙袋，以锻炼足力。

《纪效新书》中提出了大力改革和研发兵器的制器理论，指出兵器不锋利不足以战胜敌人。在这种思想的指导下，戚继光在东南沿海抗倭时积极组织部下研制新型

and bearing weight. The weapon used in the training should heavier than the actual one in the real battle. The sandbag should be tied to soldiers' legs to improve their strength.

New Theories on Military Training, Strategies and Experience, also

兵器，取得了卓越成效。一是鸟铳火药配制成功，这与当时世界上火绳枪所用的发射火药基本接轨，是中国传统火药向新型火药过渡的标志，此后各种兵书在谈到火药时，无不转载此方。二是根据当地所产的竹材制成的特殊兵器——狼筅。狼筅以大毛竹为杆，每节都有枝叶与铁制倒钩刺。狼筅由于附枝柔软，所以刀不能一下子切断，又由于它多节，所以长枪不能刺入，这种兵器在抗倭的过程中发挥了重要的作用。

mentions the importance of reforms and innovations of the weapon production. He said that if the weapon was not sharp enough, then it can not hurt the enemy. Under this guidance, Qi Jiguang invented many new-style weapons while he was in war with the Japanese pirates and gained sound effect. One is the invention of the fire case, which basically resembled the harquebus invented in other countries. It was a transitional landmark symbolizing traditional Chinese gunpowder developing into the new-style one. Since then, all the military books would quote his record when mentioned gunpowder. Two is the invention of a special weapon wolf stick made from bamboo and iron thorns. It used the bamboo stick as its body and added barbs and thorns at each section. Due to its soft nature of the branches, it can not be cut off easily. As it has many sections, so the long spear can not rival. Therefore, this weapon exerted great influence in the battles against the Japanese pirates.

明代铁炮

Iron Cannon (Ming Dynasty, 1368-1644)

《练兵实纪》

《练兵实纪》是戚继光所著的另一部有关练兵教战、制器用器的兵书，保留了《纪效新书》中行之有效的内容，又有许多发展创新之处。在此书中，戚继光依据敌情、气候、地理、守备设施和民风等客观条件进行论述，注重实效性。

此外，《练兵实纪》进一步发展了戚继光更新武器装备、改进长城守备设施的军事思想。他利用火器制造的最新成果，改制了大将军炮，创制了快枪和可以引爆地雷的机械装置，还发展了火箭技术。

Journal of Trainings

Journal of Trainings is another military book on training and weapon production, which referred the efficient content in the *New Theories on Military Training, Strategies and Experience*, and also added many original theories. In this book, Qi Jiguang states his theories according to the enemy's situation, weather, geography, defensive equipment and folk customs, etc. So it emphasizes the effectiveness.

Besides, *Journal of Trainings* also developed his military theories of renovating the weapons and promoting the defensive equipment in the Great Wall. Based on the new inventions in the firearm production, he improved the General Cannon, invented fast fire gun and the mechanical device used to ignite the mine, and improved the techniques in fire arrow production.

• 《练兵实纪》书影

Book Copy: *Journal of Trainings*

戚继光修缮长城

明朝嘉靖年间（1522—1566），北方的少数民族不断向南侵袭，迫使明朝把军事防御重点放在长城沿线。此时，东南沿海的倭寇已经平息，于是戚继光被派到蓟镇（今北京西南）修筑长城。戚继光不仅修缮了原有的主城墙，还发明了空心敌台，大大加强了长城的防御能力。空心敌台是跨长城城墙而建的中空、四面开窗的高出城墙之上的楼台，多分为上下两层，下层可供守城士兵居住，并储存武器、弹药等。敌人来袭时，士兵们便会登台迎战，与台下的守军配合作战。

• **司马台长城**

司马台长城始建于明洪武初年（1368），后又经戚继光等人修筑加固，地势险峻，工程浩繁。

Great Wall in Simatai

The Great Wall in Simatai was built in 1368 and restored and enhance by Qi Jiguang and other officers. The construction was complicated and was located at a precipitous area.

Renovation of the Great Wall, by Qi Jiguang

In 1522-1566, due to the repetitive invasions from the northern ethnic groups, the authority was forced to put the major defensive fortresses along the Great Wall. Meanwhile, the harassments from the Japanese pirates had been settled. So Qi Jiguang was appointed to Ji County (today's southwestern area of Beijing) to restore the Great Wall. Qi Jiguang repaired the original major body and invented hollow platform which greatly improved the defense capability of the Great Wall. Hollow platforms are towers built above the walls with windows on four sides. It is hollow on the inside and has two storeys. The lower storey can serve as the dormitory for the soldiers or the warehouse storing weapons and ammunition. While enemy attacked, the soldiers would climb up to the tower to confront the enemy with the soldiers below the tower.

• 空心敌台

Hollow Tower

> 《筹海图编》

明代后期，倭寇不断侵犯东南沿海地区，因此海防成了这一时期中国军事的重点。《筹海图编》就是在这一历史时期诞生的海防专著，在防倭剿倭、制器用器等方面都有精辟的论述。书中还提出了全面防倭剿倭的战略，以及建立有战斗力的海防守备部队，重视改善海防的武器装备，以制造战船为主、火器为辅的水战理论等重要海防思想。《筹海图编》是中国最早的海防专著，既总结了前人的经验，又对当时海防的筹划与建设起到了指导作用，至今仍有借鉴的价值。

作者简介

《筹海图编》的作者是明代后期著名的军事家、战略家郑若曾

> *Illustrated Collection of the Theories of Coast Defense*

In the late Ming Dynasty (1368-1644), the Japanese pirates constantly harassed the south-east coast. Therefore, in this period of time, the coast defense became an important mission in military activities. *Illustrated Collection of the Theories of Coast Defense* was completed at this time as a military canon on coast defense, which gives incisive narration on the military operations against the Japanese pirates and the weapon production. It also provides a comprehensive anti-Japanese pirates' tactic, including building an efficient coast guard force and improving the weapons and equipment for the purpose of coast defense, as well as the significant coast defense theory: warship as the main force and firearm as the auxiliary. *Illustrated Collection of the Theories of Coast*

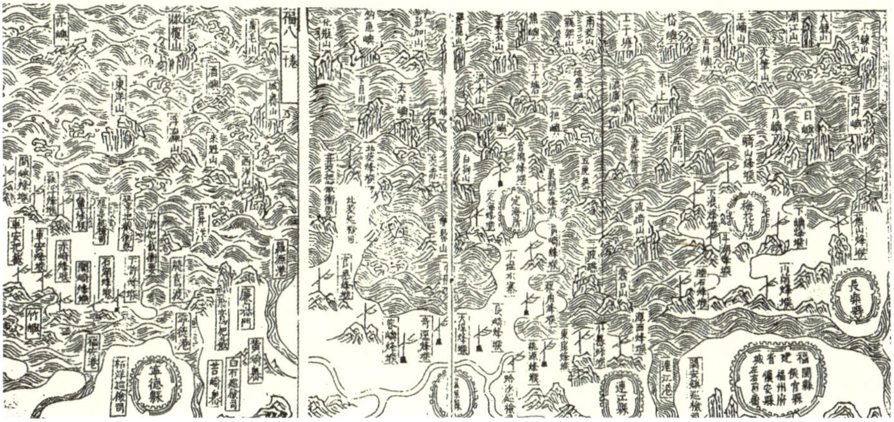

•《筹海图编》中的地形图（图片提供：FOTOE）

Terrain Map in *Illustrated Collection of the Theories of Coast Defense*

（1503—1570）。郑若曾少时好学，对天文、地理、地图、军事和政治等问题都有所研究。他一生追求学术，潜心著书，无意于仕途。他的军事著作除《筹海图编》外，还有《日本图纂》、《江南经略》等，均对后世产生了深远的影响。

主要军事思想

郑若曾在书中提出，导致倭寇灾患的根本原因是明朝当时的政治腐败、土地兼并严重、农民赋役繁重、沿海地区战备松懈等。因

Defense is the earliest treatise about coast defense, which not only concludes the former experience but also guides the defense planning and construction at that time. Today, it is still a valuable reference for academic study.

Biography

Illustrated Collection of the Theories of Coast Defense was written by a famous strategist Zheng Ruozeng (1503-1570) in the late Ming Dynasty. Zheng Ruozeng showed his talent in his early ages and dabbled in astronomy, geography, map plotting, military and politics. He dedicated his whole life in the pursuit of knowledge. He was not interested in official career and only concentrated on reading. Aside from *Illustrated Collection*

• 明代海战场景
Naval Battle (Ming Dynasty, 1368-1644)

此，防倭剿倭的根本方略是安民和备战。安民就是要委派良吏推行善政，使沿海居民安居乐业，这是巩固海防的根本保证。备战就是要加强海防建设，全歼来犯的倭寇。

《筹海图编》针对沿海抗倭作战的特点，要求将士重视沿海地形和气象对作战的影响，注意研究季风、春汛、秋汛与倭寇活动的关系。为此，书中详细列出了沿海的重要岛屿、港湾、要塞、军事要地，并绘图示意，其中的《沿海山沙图》是中国最早的沿海地图和海防图，不仅可供当时的人们

of the Theories of Coast Defense, his works also includes *Collection of Atlas and Illustrations of Japan*, *Collection of Atlas of Southern Regions* and etc., which all exerted great influence on the later generations.

Major Military Theory

Zheng Ruozeng once mentioned in his book that the reason led to the harassment of Japanese pirates was the political corruption, severe land annexation, heavy taxes and corvee and the neglected coast defense in the Ming Dynasty. Therefore, the fundamental policy of the anti-Japanese pirates was to appease the people and prepare for the war. The government should appointed upright officials to carry out the people-oriented policy to make the resident along the coast areas living a satisfied life, which was the basic assurance to consolidate the coast defense. And also the government should promote the defensive construction at coast areas to confront with the invaders.

Based on the characters of the water battle against Japanese, *Illustrated Collection of the Theories of Coast Defense* suggests that the military officer should pay attention to the influence of the coast terrain and weather and the

考查，也是后世研究明代地图的重要图籍。

郑若曾非常重视使用新型武器装备，书中记述了进犯广东的葡萄牙军队所使用的发射火药，对鸟铳的传入和仿制的情况记述也比较完备。另外还记载了当时为备倭而建造的各型战船，详细分析了它们的构造特点和战斗性能，直观地反映了当时战船建造的概况。郑若曾认为海战中御敌首先要依靠具有攻击力的大型战船，其次要凭借优势的火器。书中关于大中小型战船相编配、远中近程火器相并用的水战战术，同《纪效新书》的论述基本一致，具有鲜明的时代特色。

relationship between the Japanese pirates' activities and the season wind, spring flood and autumn flood. For this purpose, the book states the important isles, harbors, fortresses, and vital areas along the coast, and also provides many illustrations among which *Illustration of Hills and Sands Along the Coast* is the earliest coast map and defense map in China. It is not only the rare military reference, but also an important map for the research conducted by later generations.

Zheng Ruozeng emphasized the application of new weapons. The book records that the projector gunpowder used by Portugal's army who invaded Guangdong, and the introduction and imitation of the fire case. Additionally, it also depicts various warships built especially for the war against the Japanese. As in the naval battle, the main force will be the large warship and then the support of advanced firearms, so the book provides several formations of warships with different sizes and tactics of applying firearms with different ranges. The content of *Illustrated Collection of the Theories of Coast Defense* resembles the records in *New Theories on Military Training, Strategies and Experience* with distinct epochal characteristics.

> 《神器谱》

中国古代十分重视兵器的改革与创新，人们在矛、盾、刀、枪的基础上，不断扩展兵器的领域，后来发展到了火器。火器具有节省人力、射程远、威慑力大的特点，大大提升了军队的战斗力，《神器谱》就是关于火绳枪制造与使用的专著。

《神器谱》在深入研究明朝廷军事斗争战略需要的基础上，系统介绍了多种火器的制造与使用方法，根据不同的作战对象、不同的作战地域来指导火器的研制和使用。《神器谱》是一本更具科学性的著作，是明代火器发展到一个新阶段的标志。

作者简介

《神器谱》的作者是明代后期

> Collection of Military Weapons

People knew the importance of the reform and innovation of the weapons in the ancient China. On the basis of spear, shield, knife and lance, they kept extending the definition of the weapon and developed firearms which were economical on manpower, with long firing range and greater power. It greatly promoted the fighting capacity of the army. And *Collection of Military Weapons* is an academic writing about the production and instruction of harquebus.

Based on the in-depth study on the needs of the court of the Ming Dynasty in the military battles, *Collection of Military Weapons* introduces many firearms on the production method and instruction of use. It gives different advices on the manufacture and use of the firearms based on different opponents and terrains.

研究火绳枪制造与使用技术的专家赵士桢（约1553—1611）。赵士桢从小生长在海滨，家乡常遭倭寇侵袭，备受其苦，因此他非常关心海防，注重研究军事及火器技术。他研制改进了多种火器，著有《神器谱》、《神器杂说》、《神器谱或问》、《防虏车铳

Collection of Military Weapons is a scientific book, representing a new stage of the development of the firearms in the Ming Dynasty.

Biography

Collection of Military Weapons was written by Zhao Shizhen (approx. 1553-1611), an expert on the study of

• 北京保卫战

明代末年，蒙古瓦剌大军直逼北京，守卫京师的将士以城池为依靠，发挥自己火器多、装备精良的优势与敌周旋，取得了北京保卫战的胜利。

Self-defensive Battle of Beijing City

In the late Ming Dynasty, the army led by Oirat from the Mongolia grassland launched a strike over Beijing. Relying on the fortification of Beijing, the defenders in Beijing exerted their advantages in firearms and advanced weapons and equipment and successfully resisted the attack and won the battle.

议》等关于火器研制开发、使用方法的书籍。

主要军事思想

《神器谱》指出，研制神器（火器）是对国家有万世之利的大计，能使国家的军事实力迅速转弱为强，使敌人胆寒，不敢来犯，从而实现国家长治久安的目的。因此，国家需要注意增加火器的产量、提高火器的质量、改善国防设施和军队装备，官兵也必须熟悉各种火器的性能，善于使

harquebus's production and operation technique in the late Ming Dynasty. He was born in the coast area which was constantly suffered from the harassments by the Japanese pirates. Therefore, he cared about the coast defense and concentrated his study on the military strategies and firearm techniques. He invented and improved many firearms and wrote books including *Collection of Military Weapons*, *About Military Weapons*, *Questions About Collection of Military Weapons*, *Introduction of Anti-Japanese Cart*, and etc., on the development and manufacture of firearms as well as relevant training methods.

Major Military Theory

Collection of Military Weapons pointed out that the development of the firearms can benefit the country and reverse the vulnerable situation of the national military power and deter the enemy

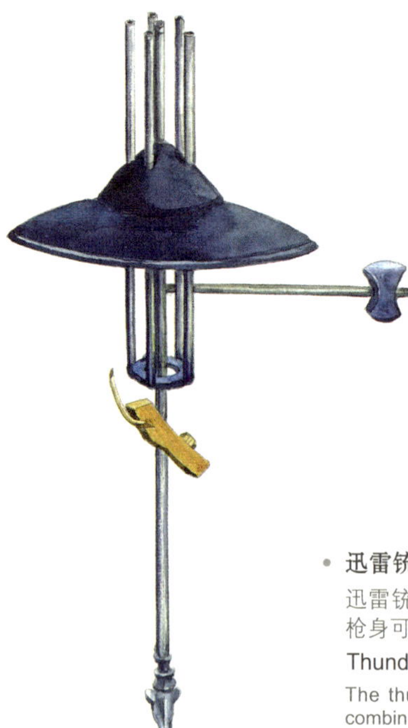

迅雷铳

迅雷铳是把五支枪身集中在一起的改良型鸟铳。由于五支枪身可连续发射弹丸，所以缩短了发射时间的间隔。

Thunder Fire Case

The thunder fire case is a developed fire case with five guns combined together. As it can fire consecutively, so it shortened the launch time.

- **明代架火战车（模型）**

架火战车造型简单，体轻灵活，三人即可操作。其中一人负责瞄准及推车，其他两人负责装填弹药和点火。使用时将几架架火战车排成队列，火箭一次齐射，杀伤力非常大。

Fire Cart of the Ming Dynasty(Model)

The fire cart is simple and motivated, which can be operated by three persons: one is in charge of aiming and pushing the cart; other two are in charge of filling ammos and launching the arrows. In the battle, several fire carts are arranged in a row and fire the arrows at the same time, which can cause huge lethality.

用各种火器。

《神器谱》认为，研制火器必须因时而创新，出奇制胜。他还要求火器制造部门选用技精艺熟的工匠来制造精利的枪炮，不可有丝毫

from further harassment and attain the purpose of maintaining a prolonged stability. Therefore, the government should increase the output of the firearms and raise the quality and improve the defensive instrument as well as the military equipment. And the soldiers and officers should also study the property of different firearms and learn to handle all kinds of firearms.

Collection of Military Weapons, states that the development of firearms should focus on the innovation due to the fickle circumstances. The author also

虎头木牌（模型）

明代发明的一种形似盾牌的火器，牌上设孔，装有火铳和火箭等。

Tiger-head Wood Shield (Model)

It was a firearm invented in the Ming Dynasty with firing holes in it and installed fire cases or fire arrows.

差错。书中还指出，使用火器时必须灵活多变，只有因时、因敌、因地而变，才能达到取胜的目的。因时而变是指作战时要适时捕捉战机，不可因滥战而失去应有的作战效果。因敌而变就是要根据不同敌人的不同作战特点，采取不同的火器。因地而变就是在不同的地形作战时，要使用不同的火器。

raised that the production of firearms should be conducted by skillful craftsmen as the gun and cannon can not tolerate any errors. As to the operation of the firearms, it says that the tactics should be flexible based on the changes of time, opponent and terrain to seize the victory. Based on the change of time indicates the leader should know how to take the opportunity to achieve the best result. Based on the change of opponent indicates the leader should apply different firearms to deal with the opponents with different operation patterns. Based on the change of terrain indicates the leader should apply different firearms based on various terrains.

平壤之战

平壤之战是中国历史上利用火器的优势而取得胜利的重要战争实例。明万历二十年（1592），日本发兵进攻朝鲜，企图侵占平壤。明廷应朝鲜国王的请求，命李如松率兵四万余援朝。在这场战争中，明军装备了大量火炮，而日军普遍装备的是鸟铳，与明军的火力相比处于弱势。中朝联军以火力优势歼敌万余人，收复了许多失地，日本被迫退至朝鲜东南沿海一隅。

Battle of Pingrang

Battle of Pingrang is an important military operation in which the firearms exerted the advantages and laid the foundation of the victory in Chinese history. In 1592, Japanese invaded the Korea with intention of taking the capital city Pingrang. At the request of the Korean king, Ming Dynasty sent Li Rusong along with 40,000 soldiers to rescue the Pingrang City. In the battle, Ming's army was equipped numerous firearms while the simple fire case was the major weapon of Japanese. Due to the unbalanced firepower, the joint army of Ming and Korea killed thousands of Japanese soldiers and recovered many lost lands. And Japanese was chased down to the southeastern area at the coast.

- **虎蹲炮**

  虎蹲炮是明嘉靖年间出现的火炮，射程虽不远，但机动灵活，适于山地作战，曾大量装备作战部队。

  Crouching Tiger Cannon

  It appeared in the Jiajing Period (1522-1566) in the Ming Dynasty. Although the firing range was not long enough, it was very motive and fit for the mountain battle. It was equipped in the army in large scale.

> 《武备志》

《武备志》是中国古代兵学宝库中规模最大、篇幅最多、内容最全面的兵学巨著，设类详尽，编纂方法科学，被兵家誉为古典兵学的百科全书。它是在明代后期东南沿海外患丛生、北方游牧民族不断向明廷挑战的严峻军事形势下，由茅元仪在总结历代兵学成就的基础上，针对当时军事斗争的需要编撰而成的。全书共240卷，约200万字，配有图片738幅。

作者简介

《武备志》由明末将领茅元仪（1594—1640）所辑。茅元仪擅长用兵之道，熟悉用兵方略，一生著述宏富，包括《武备志》、《督师纪略》、《复辽砭语》、《暇老

> Book of Military Theory

Book of Military Theory is a military canon with the largest scale, longest narration, and the most comprehensive content. It has detailed categories and is compiled with reasonable methods. So it is praised as the Military Encyclopedia in ancient China. It was written by Mao Yuanyi in the late Ming Dynasty when the pirates were raging at the southeast coast and ethnic groups constantly attacked from the north. Based on the former military theories, Mao Yuanyi compiled this canon in the demand for developing the national military power. The book includes 240 chapters and more than 2,000,000 characters as well as 738 illustrations.

Biography

Book of Military Theory was written by the general Mao Yuanyi (1594-

斋杂记》、《野航史话》，《石民赏心集》、《江村集》等六十多部典籍。

主要军事思想

针对当时重文轻武的社会现象，茅元仪在书中提出了文武并重的主张。他以史为例，坚持文武并重的主张，其中文事指政治，武事指军队和国防建设。他建议朝廷大力整军经武，训练兵马，从各方面做好御敌作战的准备。

茅元仪在《武备志》中充分分析了明代国防的特点：明代后期，西北边防和江防都受到了严重威胁，而这些地方的守备设施又因多年没有修缮而防备力大大下降。为此，书中提出要大力加强边防建设，着重加强边、海、江的防御能力。茅元仪认为边防的重点在土地广袤的西北地区，应加强选将练兵，建造堡垒，以保护边疆人民的安全。海防的重点在东南沿海，应重视日本侵犯中国的野心。江防也不能忽视，它与边防和海防是同等重要的。

《武备志》中提出了火器要因

1640) in the late Ming Dynasty. Mao Yuanyi excelled in the military theories and strategies. He wrote more than 60 books, including *Book of Military Theory*, *Notes on Training*, *Comments on Liao's Restoration*, *Notes of Free Man Study*, *History of Wild Sailing*, *Appreciation Notes of Rock Collectors*, and *Collection of River Villages*.

Major Military Theory

As the military specialist earned less social recognition than literati, Mao Yuanyi pointed out the opinion on balanced development. Based on several historical cases, he insisted on the importance of the military education (military development and defensive construction) resembled the significance of the literary education (politics). He suggested the authority to reorganize the army and train the war horses to prepare the war from each aspect.

Mao Yuanyi analyzed the characters of the national defense of the Ming Dynasty in his book: in the late Ming Dynasty, the frontiers in the northwestern areas and the riverside fortresses were under severe threat. And the defensive instruction at these places was in low performance due to the lack of renovation

冬船
Winter Boat

开浪船
Swing Boat

哨船
Scout Boat

• 《武备志》中记述的各种战船
Various Warships Documented in *Book of Military Theory*

情而用的三个原则：第一是因时而用，即统兵将领要根据天象、气候等天时情况选用火器，例如我军处于上风时，可选用火箭、火球等；第二是因地而用，即统兵将领要善于根据地形来选择火器，例如在平原上要选用射程较远的火器；第三是因敌而用，即统兵将领要善于根

for many years. Therefore, he suggested the government should enhance the frontier construction and develop the defensive capability at the coast areas and riverside. And the priority should be given to the vast northwestern areas. Selecting talented officers and soldiers and building fortresses were the major approaches to protect the people at the frontiers. As to the coast defense, the emphasis should be placed in the southeastern coast areas. And the soldiers and officers must be alerted to Japan's ambition. And the riverside defense also could not be neglected, as it was as important as the coast defense.

Book of Military Theory mentions three principles on the operation of firearms: the first is to apply the firearms based on the weather conditions. For example, if the home side was in advantage, the fire arrow and fire ball will be good options. The second is to apply the firearms based on the terrain. For example, the long-ranged firearm

一窝蜂（模型）

一窝蜂是一种多发火箭，一次可发射32支。

Hive-shaped Fire Arrow(Model)

The hive-shaped fire arrow is a type of arrow launching device with 32 firing barrels.

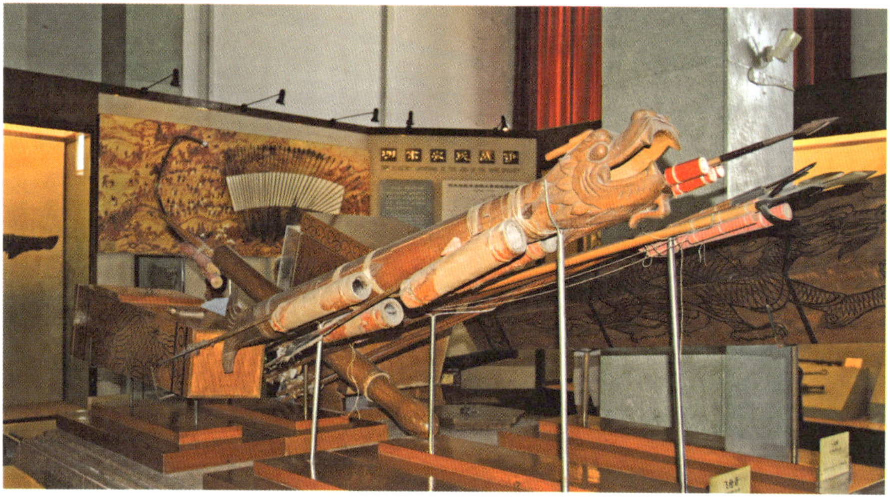

• **火龙出水（模型）**

这是一种水陆两用的火箭，龙腹内装有数支火箭，龙头与龙尾各装有两个火箭筒。战斗时，在距离地面三四尺处点燃引信，火箭立刻腾空飞出，飞行距离可达1500米远。当4支引信燃烧将尽时，便会点燃龙腹内的火箭，数支火箭会从龙口中喷射而出，直达目标。

Fire Dragon in the Water (Model)

It is an amphibian arrow launching device, with multiple fire arrows installed inside the dragon belly and two rocket launchers respectively installed in the dragon head and tail. In the battle, after the fuse is ignited when the device is 3-4 *Chi* (1 *Chi*=1/3 meter) above the land, the fire arrows will fly through the launchers and are able to travel 1,500 meters. When the four fuses are about quenched, the fire arrows stored in the dragon belly will be ignited and then multiple fire arrows will come out of the dragon's mouth and hit the target.

据不同的敌情而使用不同的火器，例如在守城时要用威力较大的火器来攻击敌人。因此，拥有种类繁多的火器并不代表着战争一定能够取得胜利，关键还在于将领和士兵能否在战争中根据实际情况运用各种火器。

is fit in the battle on the plain. The third is to apply the firearms based on the opponents. For example, the city defender should apply large firearms with powerful firepower to attack the enemy. Therefore, the variety of firearms doesn't guarantee the victory. The key is in the practical operation conducted by the officers and soldier.

> 《海国图志》

《海国图志》是一部介绍世界地理、历史、军事知识的综合性图书，记述了世界各国的历史、地理、政治、经济、军事和科学技术，乃至宗教、文化等情况，并配有世界地图、各大洲地图和各国地图等。该书是在清代政治家、思想家林则徐主持编译的《四洲志》的基础上增补而成的。《海国图志》传播了西方近代自然科学知识，记述了西方社会的文化、制度和风土人情，拓宽了中国人的视野，开辟了近代中国向西方学习的新风气。《海国图志》问世后，在当时爱国官兵和文人学士中产生了强烈的影响，书中的军事地理思想和海防思想成为清代后期推行军事自强国策的思想武器。

> Records and Maps of the World

Records and Maps of the World is a comprehensive canon introducing the foreign geography and military knowledge. It includes the history of the foreign countries, geography, politics, economy, military affairs, science and technology, as well as religion and culture, being accompanied with maps of the world, continents and countries. This book was compiled based on the book *Geography of the World* (*Si Zhou Zhi*) compiled and translated by Lin Zexu, a famous politician and scholar in the Qing Dynasty. *Records and Maps of the World* brought the modern natural science and the western culture, system and customs to China, broadened Chinese vision and initiated a new prevalence of learning from the West. After the publication of *Records and Maps of the World*, the book

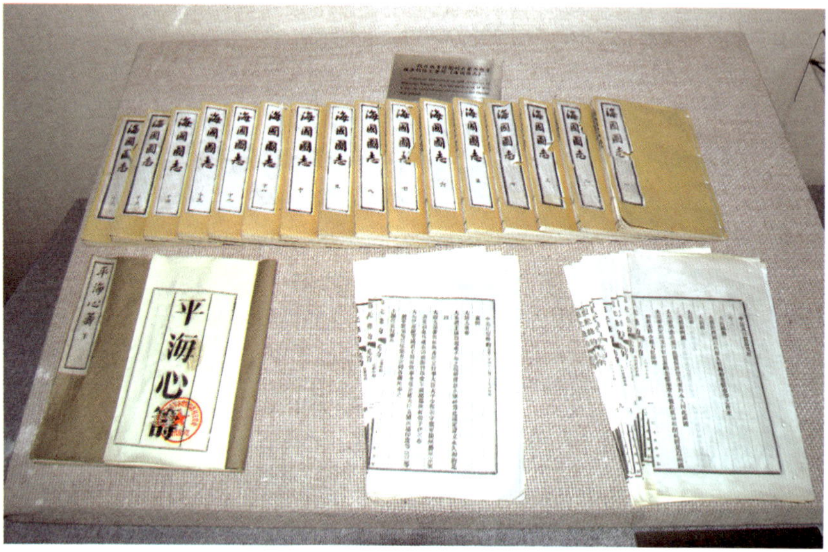

• 《海国图志》书影（图片提供：微图）
Book Copy: *Records and Maps of the World*

作者简介

《海国图志》的作者是清代启蒙思想家、政治家魏源（1794—1857）。魏源所倡导的“师夷之长技以制夷”激励了无数中国的有识之士，并在一定程度上加大了中国近代化的进程。魏源不仅仅是清代后期进步的思想家、史学家、文学家，同时也是一位优秀的军事理论家，《海国图志》就全面反映了其军事地理思想和海防思想。魏源的

exerted great influence on the patriotic officers and soldiers as well as literati. The theories of the military geography and coast defense in this book became the major guiding thought in the later reform in the late Qing Dynasty (1644-1911)

Biography

Records and Maps of the World was written by Wei Yuan (1794-1857), a famous ideologist and politician in the Qing Dynasty. Wei Yuan's opinion of "mastering the skills of the barbarians to

• 魏源塑像
Statue of Wei Yuan

著作很多，除《海国图志》外，还有《书古微》、《诗古微》、《默觚》、《老子本义》、《孙子集注》等。

主要军事思想

《海国图志》的主旨为“师夷之长技以制夷”。意思是向西方学习先进的技术，以抵抗他们的侵略。书中从介绍西方世界的历史地理入手，进而介绍西方高超的武器

subdue themselves” inspired numerous scholars and promoted the progress of the modernization in modern China. Wei Yuan was not only an enlightened ideologist, historian and writer, as well as an outstanding military theorist in China. *Records and Maps of the World* fully reflects his theories on military geography and coast defense. Aside from *Records and Maps of the World*, Wei Yuan wrote many books, including *Shu Gu Wei, Shi Gu Wei, Mo Gu, Original Theories in Lao Zi*, and *Collection of the Annotations of Master Sun's Art of War*, etc.

Major Military Theory

The main point in the book *Records and Maps of the World* is mastering the skills of the barbarians to subdue themselves, meaning to learn the advanced technique from the Western people. It starts from the introduction on the world history and geography and concentrates on the Western weapon production techniques. Wei Yuan thought the West possessed three advanced skills: warships, firearms and training methods. Therefore, in order to develop the national military power, Chinese should study the Western technologies in shipbuilding and firearms production as well as the training

• 清代神威无敌大将军炮

此大将军炮为铜质，于清康熙十五年（1676）制造，炮重1137千克，炮身长2.48米，口径110 毫米，每次可装填1.5—2公斤火药，炮弹重3—4千克。

Invincible Mighty General Cannon (Qing Dynasty, 1644-1911)

This copper cannon was built in 1675, weighed 1,137 kg, with a length of 2.48 m and 110 mm caliber. It can be filled with 1.5-2 kg gunpowder and fire 3-4 kg cannonball.

• 清代将领装束

Officer's Military Uniform (Qing Dynasty, 1644-1911)

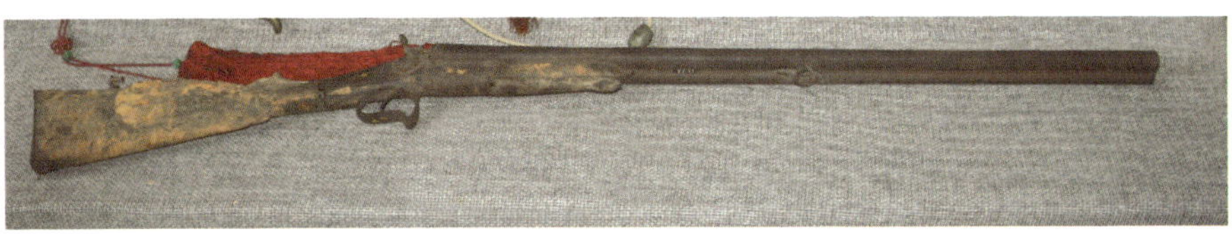

• 清代奇枪

奇枪是清代前期制造的一种后装火绳枪，有底，底侧有火孔，内装弹药。

Qing's Rifle

The Qing's rifle is a type of back loading harquebus produced in the early Qing Dynasty, with a base and a fire hole below to store the ammo.

制造技术，认为西方的长技有三：一是战舰，二是火器，三是练兵、养兵之法。因此要振兴国家的武备，就要了解和学习西方建战舰、造火器，以及选兵、练兵的方法。魏源在《海国图志》中，集纳了当时国内外著名军事技术人员的研究成果，尤其是对西方的枪、炮、舰船和水雷、地雷等进行了研究。

针对当时中国不断有西方国家从沿海入侵的情况，书中提出了“以守为战”的海防思想。主张避

methods. In the *Records and Maps of the World*, it includes the research results in military technology at home and abroad, especially the Western gun, cannon, warship and naval mine and land mine.

Facing the constant invasions from the Western world, the book raised a thought of coast defense which was to take the defense as the attack. It advocated avoiding the opponent's advantages of having warships and efficient firearms and choosing the appropriate terrain, selecting skillful

清代战船（模型）
Warship in the Qing Dynasty(Model)

开西方坚船利炮和海上作战的优势，选择有利的地形，选练壮兵，埋伏奇兵，备好火攻，诱敌深入，打击夷兵。还主张裁撤部分旧式水师，购置一些中小型战舰，组建一支能在外海抗敌的新舰队。

此外，书中还主张建设船厂和炮厂可与兴办民用工业相结合。造船厂不仅可以制造战舰，还可以建造商船，供运输货物之用。火器局在制造枪炮之余，还制造量天尺、千里镜、火轮机、千斤秤等对国计民生有用的东西。

soldiers and relying on the strategies to lure the enemy into the fire ambush. It also suggested that the government should decrease part of the old naval army and purchase several middle-sized or small-sized warships to build a new-style warship troop to resist the foreign attack.

Furthermore, the book also proposed to build the shipyard and cannon factory to promote the development of civil industry. The shipyard can produce warships and merchant ships for cargo delivery. Aside from the firearms, the Firearm Bureau also can produce military ruler, telescope, fire engine and large scale for people's livelihood.

China Stones 中国石
Huizhou Art 徽州艺术
剪纸

中国红系列

中国印
老茶具
笔墨纸砚
书法
中国饮食
古镇
古钱币
徽州艺术
紫砂壶
吉祥图案
古代兵器
古典建筑
中医
西藏艺术
佛像艺术
古铜器
梅兰竹菊
传统乐器
长城
年画
古代服饰
剪纸
中国画
中国酒
唐诗
中国节日
中国石
少数民族服饰
中国雕刻
中国扇

Chinese Red Series

传统手工艺
Traditional Handicraft

中国色彩
Chinese Colors

刺绣
Embroidery

中国禅
Chinese Zen Buddhism

中国棋艺
Art of Chinese Board Games

宋词
Ci-poems of the Song Dynasty

茶马古道
Ancient Tea-Horse Road

中国名湖
Famous Lakes in China

中国料器
Chinese Glassware

帝王陵寝
Royal Mausoleums in China

中华传统美德
Traditional Virtues of China

中国姓氏
Chinese Surnames

传统家具
Traditional Chinese Furniture

中国名山
Famous Mountains in China

中国染织
Chinese Dyeing and Weaving

武术
Chinese Martial Arts

民间玩具
Folk Toys

中国古代教育
Education in Ancient China

中国神话传说
Chinese Mythology and Legends

中国传统游戏
Chinese Traditional Games

四大名著
China's Four Great Classic Novels

中国古代科学
Science in Ancient China

金银器
Gold and Silver Articles

竹木牙角器
Art Crafts Made of Bamboo, Wood, Ivory and Horn

风筝
Kites

中国盆景
Chinese Bonsai

景泰蓝
Cloisonné

泥塑
Clay Sculpture

面塑
Dough Modeling

大运河
The Grand Canal

中国历史名城
Historical and Famous Cities in China

中国结
Chinese Knot

秦陵与兵马俑
The Mausoleum of Qin Shi Huang and Terracotta Warriors

皮影
Shadow Play

古代帝王
Ancient Emperors

中国陶器
Chinese Pottery

中国漆器
Chinese Lacquerware

中国名寺
Famous Temples in China

中国石窟
Chinese Grottoes

中国古桥
Chinese Ancient Bridges

中国名塔
Famous Pagodas in China

中国民居
Chinese Civil Residents

民间戏曲
Chinese Folk Opera

中国灯彩
Chinese Lanterns

诸子百家
The Hundred Schools of Thought

中国牌坊
Chinese Memorial Archways

中国茶艺
Tea Art in China

秦砖汉瓦
Qin Bricks and Han Tiles

面具
Masks

颐和园
The Summer Palace

鼻烟壶
Snuff Bottle

丝绸之路
Silk Road

汉字
Chinese Characters

中国木偶艺术
Art of Chinese Puppetry

古代兵书
Ancient Books on the Art of War

道教文化
Culture of the Taoism

古代交通
Ancient Transport

古代壁画
Ancient Chinese Mural Painting

古代衡器
Ancient Weighing Apparatus

二十四节气
Twenty-four Solar Terms

中国名泉
Famous Springs in China

长江黄河
The Yangtze River and the Yellow River

中国杂技
Chinese Acrobatics

中国婚俗
Wedding Customs in China

匾额楹联
Inscribed Boards and Couplets

中国建筑装饰
Chinese Architectural Decoration

十二生肖
Chinese Zodiac Signs

古代佩饰
Accessories Wore by Ancient Chinese

文房清供
Stationery and Bibelot in Ancient Studies

中国瑞兽祥禽
Auspicious Animals and Birds in Chinese Culture